DIRECTLY TRANSLATED
FROM THE DEAD SEA SCROLLS:

And when they bless all the men who are on God's side, those, that is, who walk uprightly in all His ways, the priests shall say:

> "May He bless you with all that is good,
> and deliver you from every evil.
> May he clarify your mind to understand life,
> And permit you to experience Eternity,
> And there turn to you His loving face
> For your happiness forever."

> —Benedictions (Column II)
> Manual of Discipline

As long as I live it shall be a rule engraved on my tongue to bring praise like fruit for an offering and my lips as a sacrificial gift. I will make skilful music with lyre and harp to serve God's glory, and the flute of my lips will I raise in praise of His rule of righteousness. Both morning and evening I shall enter into the Covenant of God: and at the end of both I shall recite His commandments, and so long as they continue to exist, there will be my frontier and my journey's end.

Therefore I will bless His name in all I do, before I move hand or foot, whenever I go out or come in, when I sit down and when I rise, even when lying on my couch I will chant His praise.

My lips shall praise Him as I sit at the table which is set for all, and before I lift my hand to partake of any nourishment from the delicious fruits of the earth.

When fear and terror come, and there is only anguish and distress, I will still bless and thank Him for His wondrous deeds, and meditate upon His power, and lean upon His mercies all day long. For I know that in His hand is justice for all that live, and all His works are true. So, when trouble comes, or salvation, I praise Him just the same.

> —Praising God at All Times (Column X)
> Manual of Discipline

The LOST YEARS of JESUS REVEALED

BY THE REV. DR. CHARLES FRANCIS POTTER
B.D., S.T.M., LITT. D.

Unitarian minister & humanist

NEWLY REVISED SECOND EDITION

*provocative speculation on implications
of these newly discovered Dead Sea Scrolls,
1958, 1962*

A FAWCETT GOLD MEDAL BOOK

FAWCETT PUBLICATIONS, INC., GREENWICH, CONN.
MEMBER OF AMERICAN BOOK PUBLISHERS COUNCIL, INC.

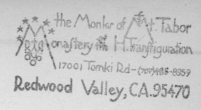

Contents

The Lost Years
of Jesus
Revealed

of the Temple that would very likely
Jewish day of atonement. . . . Was this man a
ally preacher who . . . [illegible]
out all in a certain . . . [illegible]

1. The New Jesus

The translation and preliminary study of hundreds of priceless ancient manuscripts, lately and simultaneously discovered—an Essene library in Palestine and a Gnostic one in Egypt—has already revealed to startled and still secretive scholars, but not yet to the working clerics and laity of the Christian world, a new Jesus—an impressive personality of greater mental stature, deeper wisdom, and wider experience than has hitherto been claimed by his worshipers or suspected by his critics.

It is a different Jesus who now emerges from behind the quaint legends and contradictory oral traditions of the disciples, from the "cloud which received him out of their sight;" He is no longer the Christ created by their credulity and transformed into one more typical virgin-born and bodily-resurrected pagan deity by the busy creed-manufacturing theologians of succeeding centuries.

(The new "demythologized" Jesus, seen from afar, is already stampeding the more canny modern theologians to the new ark of safety, the Barth-Bultmann Bandwagon, where they chant the new Christian (?) mantra, "The Resurrection was not something that happened to Jesus, but something that happened to the faith of his disciples." In other words, the myth of the Resurrection still saves, if you have faith enough to believe that myth is sometimes closer to truth than is history.)

But, on the other hand, neither is the New Jesus the uneducated faith-healer and miracle-monger of Galilee, alleged by materialistic rationalist critics to have spoken

9

only colloquial Aramaic (the first Yiddish), to have written only on the ground with his finger, and to have been quite ignorant of the wonderful Greek paideia and Roman civilization of his time.

The New Jesus appearing at last out of the various "clouds of unknowing," is surprising even those who have long hoped for some such Second Coming of the Son of Man. Careful study of the Essene Scrolls from the caves by the Salty Sea, confirmed by the Egyptian Gnostic codices from Nag-Hammadi, reveals him to have been not only well-versed in the knowledge and culture of Rome, Persia, Athens and Alexandria, a wide traveler and a great teacher, but also an original, independent thinker and a dedicated existential empiricist (in the midst of absolutists), ever deliberately seeking new truth by observation and experiment, even unto death.

The first edition of *The Lost Years of Jesus Revealed*, which had two printings totaling more than 200,000 copies, was widely welcomed. Hundreds of letters have reached publisher and author, mostly appreciative and grateful for information not otherwhere available. One irate woman, however, a "kiver-to-kiver" literalist, wrote that she had burned the book, but demanded her fifty cents back—from the author! But a world-circling fellow-clergyman wrote from Cairo that, the week before, at a Benares bookstall, he had seen people "lined up" to buy the paperback.

It seems that many Hindus believe that Jesus' "Lost Years" were, partly at least, spent in India, getting much of his best teaching from the Vedas. Didn't he say, "Take my yoga upon you and learn of me, for my yoga is easy"? (Both yoga and yoke are pronounced as one syllable, with final vowel silent, and both are the same word, zeugos, in Greek.)

Fanciful as it may seem to an American, the thought of any connection between Jesus' teachings and India is rendered less fantastic not only by the scrolls from the Qumran caves, but especially by the new find of many Gnostic Christian books in Egypt.

But these codices from Nag-Hammadi deserve a chapter by themselves, for it is beginning to look as if Jesus may have taken a boat from Joppa to Alexandria. (See Chapter 17.)

I appreciate the help I have received in writing this book, help either from inspiration or indignation, derived from well over 300 books and as many articles in theological journals and reviews, dealing with the Qumran manuscripts, the Nag-Hammadi codices, the history of the "interbiblical period," the rise and decline of apocalypticism, the provenance and proliferation of Gnosticism, the interaction of Christianity and the Greek paideia, the background, education, and personality of Jesus, and the origins of Essenism and Christianity, together especially with the effect of Essenism on Jesus and his legacy to Christianity. These books and articles are too numerous to be mentioned here, but I shall include in the next book of this Dead Sea Scrolls trilogy an up-to-date bibliography, considerably expanded from the lists already published in my several articles in the *Library Journal* and *Publishers' Weekly*. But I must mention with gratitude the assistance I have had from the various volumes by each of the following fearless and honest scholars: Drs. Dupont-Sommer, Albright, Allegro, Schubert, Black, Jaeger, F. C. and R. M. Grant, F. L. and F. M. Cross, Grobel, Quispel, Doresse, Freedman, Enslin, Parker, Goodenough, Morton Smith, Muilenburg, Bo Reicke, van Unnik, Gilmour, R. de Vaux, Milik, Bultmann, Cullman, Schweitzer, Harnack, and their pioneering predecessors, Dillman, Ewald, Holtzmann, Schürer, R. H. Charles, Cheyne, and Ernst Renan, now coming at last into his own.

11

2. The Challenge to Christianity

It was in 1945, we now know, that the secret caves of the great Essene library, miscalled the "Dead Sea Scrolls," were accidentally discovered by Bedouin nomads in the wady Qumran, about fourteen miles from Jerusalem. Since then, enough of the rolled leather and copper cylinders, and the tens of thousands of fragments of hundreds of manuscripts, have been deciphered and translated for the scholars and theologians to know, even if the American lay public does not, that the proven Mother of Christianity was the splinter Jewish sect sometimes called Essenes.

We know, if we have read the reports in French, German and Hebrew scientific journals, that these pre-Christian Essenes must be accorded priority on much that has hitherto been thought original in Christianity. Their scriptures, not accredited in our Bible, can be read (and have been) in Christian Sunday morning services of worship without the congregations' suspecting the substitution.

A century or more before the Christian New Testament was written, the Qumran Essenes were familiar with the ideas, teachings, proverbs, prayers, beatitudes, blessings, and even the beautiful sentences in Jesus' Sermon on the Mount, which he was quoting from Essene Scrolls, as he and his audience knew, though we may not. Even the preaching of the Gospel, the Good News, or, as the now current theological phrase has it, the "kerygma" of Kingdom Come, was evidently out of Qumran by John the

Baptist, as well as the baptism wherewith he baptized Jesus "to fulfill all righteousness," a key Essenian phrase. And the very name of the Christian Bible, the New Testament, came from these monks of Qumran, who never called themselves Essenes, but the "Sons of Zadok" (King David's high priest), or, significantly, the Community of the New Covenant. And "New Covenant" was a better word to translate the Aramaic word which Christians later translated as "New Testament."

At Jesus' last meal with his disciples, which resembled more a ritual bread and wine communion of Essenes anticipating the messianic meal of the Coming Kingdom than it did a Passover, it will be remembered that Jesus raised the "cup of the New Covenant" in true Essenic fashion, promising his disciples they would eat and drink with him in his coming kingdom.

Hundreds of other evidences of the Essene origin of the ideas, beliefs, and teachings of Jesus, John the Baptist, John the Disciple, Paul, and the other New Testament writers have been noted by the scholars working on the Scrolls. Some will be considered later in this book.

And now that the proven Mother of Christianity is known to have been the prior Community of the New Covenant commonly called the Essenes, the momentous question challenging the conscience of all Christendom is whether the child will have the grace, courage, and honesty to acknowledge and honor its own mother!

That is the challenge to Christianity this book makes!

To date, the theologians have had time enough to tell their communicants the epochal significance of the findings of the Essene library, but their utterances have been —especially in America—singularly hesitant, reluctant, and incomplete. Some distort the meaning of the Scrolls for their own purposes. Others are waiting a generation or two before making up their minds!

13

Devout religionists of more than one faith rejoiced when the Scrolls were first discovered, thinking God Himself must have preserved the copies of such Bible books as Isaiah, manuscripts a thousand years older than any previously known; but the enthusiasm cooled when they learned that other Scrolls, dating a century before Jesus, contained sayings they had thought original with him.

The laity are alarmed, fearing that somehow the Dead Sea manuscripts will undermine their orthodox faith, and their fear is not at all allayed by the assurances soothingly given them by the scholars they call "hired critics," whom they distrust anyway.

This alarm of good Christians is amusingly illustrated in the anecdote of the pious little girl who came home from Sunday School where talk had circulated about the pastor's sermon on the Scrolls. Excitedly, the child declared she was never going back again. "Why, dear?" asked her mother. The little girl said that her teacher said that Jesus was a Jew. "Never mind, darling," comforted her mother. "It may be true, but everybody knows that God is a good Presbyterian."

The gradual spreading of information as to the nature and significance of the Qumran cave finds, however, cannot be prevented and will most certainly set the woods afire in rural America and disturb all of our church-going people. The scholars who are saying that the Scrolls will make no difference with Christian doctrine because Christianity has already accepted the scientific historical point-of-view just do not know their U.S.A. One has only to remember that the latest attempt to repeal the anti-evolution law in Tennessee was defeated by a majority vote larger than that by which the original law was passed! Witness, too, that the fastest growing sects today are in the Fundamentalist wing.

When the sincere and earnest orthodox people who make up the great majority of American Christians are told that the newly discovered Scrolls, plus the other non-

Biblical books they never heard of, like Enoch and Jubilees, have made out-of-date the King James and every
other version of the Bible—Christian or Jewish—there is
going to be a religious controversy more hotly contested
than the Modernist-Fundamentalist debates and the
Scopes Evolution Trial of the 1920's. Which reminds me
that when Darrow, Hays, and the other defense lawyers
attempted to introduce a copy of the Hebrew Bible into
the evidence of that trial, along with the English Douay-
Rheims, American Standard, and the Moffatt translations,
the Fundamentalists were amazed. One of them said in
my hearing, "What right the Jews have got to have a
Bible, I'd like to know!" It is also on the record that a
lawyer on that side wanted it understood that in Tennessee when anyone mentioned the Bible, the only one
meant was "the old original *Saint* James Bible." [Italics
mine.]

Imagine telling him that the Essene Scrolls will show
many of his sacred and trusted Bible chapters to be in-
accurate, garbled, and both expurgated and interpolated,
theologically. Try and tell him, or any other Fundamentalist, that the famous verse in the Book of Habakkuk, "The
just shall live by his faith," which Paul interpreted to
mean faith in Jesus Christ, and on which Martin Luther
launched the Protestant Reformation, was originally interpreted a century before Paul by an Essene commentator to mean faith in the Essene Teacher of Righteousness. You will meet first incredulity and then belligerency!

There is hardly a book in the Old Testament that will
not need corrections and improved readings in the light
of the Qumran manuscripts, nor a New Testament book
that will not suffer considerable reinterpretation of key
verses on which doctrines depend. Few believing Christians yet realize (for few scholars are yet admitting) how
many ·important doctrines are due to be changed radi-
cally, and how many others should eventually be eliminated when the Scrolls are properly recognized and

evaluated in relation to the New Testament. The very vulnerable doctrine of the Holy Spirit will have to go, as we shall see, and will take with it inevitably the doctrine of the Trinity, which was never in the Bible anyway.

Moreover, there are many psalms, prayers, benedictions, graces before meat, collections of messianic passages, "bouquets" of comforting scripture verses, and even whole books once accepted as holy scripture by Christians and Jews, and later rejected by both when they came to hate each other, which should now be added to our Bible!

The Essenes, you see, were the intermediate step between Judaism and Christianity, and when the Jews and Christians came to hate each other, due largely to the charge by Gentile Christians that the Jews were "Christ-killers," both sides turned on the Essenes and eliminated the Essene religious literature from their canonical scriptures as far as possible, or prevented its inclusion. The Jews would not let Enoch and similar apocalyptical books be included in their canon because they were too Christian and had been quoted too frequently by Christians in support of the new doctrines. And the Christians, in turn, rejected Enoch later as too Jewish.

Today, if Jews and Christians both were magnanimous, forgiving, and brotherly enough, the Essene literature, which really belongs in the rich Judeo-Christian religious heritage, might afford a means of reconciliation and friendly co-operation to meet world problems.

For the pioneer quality in Essenism, so little understood by outsiders in that day, included the then-very-novel idea of democracy in religion. We are now so used to fraternal organizations that we can hardly realize what an impact Essenism made when it was "the first form of organized monasticism in the Mediterranean world."

Essenism was really a revolutionary new form of social order, an ideal co-operative commonwealth in miniature. The more progressive Jewish leaders had come to recognize that the failure of the old monarchy, when the nation was led into the Babylonian captivity, had been duplicated by the failure of the new Hasmonean rulers after the Maccabean uprising in the second century B.C. In that crisis came a new leader with a new idea.

The Zadokite Document of The Admonition, one of the discovered Essene books, tells (i:ll) how bewildered the people were, blindly groping their way until God "raised up for them a righteous teacher to lead them in the way of His heart."

The original and surprising thing about this heaven-sent Teacher of Righteousness was that his new co-operative, communitarian brotherhood, with a new priesthood on the ancient Zadokite pattern, not only met the immediate need of the time, but was the first religious society to establish and observe the sacraments of baptism and the eucharistic meal, and, most advanced of all, was the first group to condemn and abolish the age-old institution of human slavery.

The Teacher of Righteousness was not the first pacifist in history, but he was the first to implement his peace theories with an over-all practical measure which, if generally adopted, would abolish war. He taught his Essene brotherhood not to manufacture any weapons and, according to Philo, would not allow within the Qumran community "any maker of arrows, spears, swords, nor any manufacturer of engines of war, nor any man occupied with a military avocation, or even with peaceful practices which might easily be converted to mischief."

Philo, Josephus, and Pliny, all contemporary historians, praise the Essenes highly, as we shall show later, but there is another quotation from Philo concerning the co-operative brotherhood which is appropriate to mention here because it may have influenced Jesus. In his *Every Virtuous Man Is Free*," Philo, after praising these men "who live naturally and reasonably, and are so free that they inspire their neighbors also with the spirit of freedom," goes on to "beg them to come out to us and pacify our too

17

turbulent and troubled lives, preaching to us to substitute for our wars and slavery and unspeakable evils their gospel of peace and freedom, and an abundance of their other rich blessings."

Now it was during the young manhood of Jesus that Philo wrote this plea for the self-segregated saints to come out and preach their gospel in the marketplace. Did Jesus hear or read and then accept the challenge? Was he a member of the Essene brotherhood at the time? Some scholars say that Jesus could not have been one because the Essenes were secluded monastics who had fled the world, while he walked among men and even consorted with publicans and sinners. But could he not have been a student in the Qumran library, or even a member of the brotherhood, for many years, and then, having heard Philo's call or some other, and stimulated by his own sensitive conscience, have come out into the marketplace to preach his own somewhat revised and improved version of the Essene gospel?

It is a difficult task today to separate what was new and original in Jesus' teaching from what he learned from the Essenes and from the other Jews, and perhaps from Greeks as well. It is also difficult to discover his own teachings underneath the accumulated layers of theological accretions and changes made by his followers.

Naturally, the excitement and controversy over the discovery of the remnants of the great Essene library will subside sufficiently for sober, honest men to sit down and appraise without prejudice the manuscripts and assembled fragments in their relation to the Christian literature, canonical and other, of the late first and second centuries A.D. Only then will it be appropriate to inquire long and seriously whether or not the Christian Church of those two centuries was any great improvement in its literature, rituals, doctrines, morals, and practices over the Essene Community of the New Covenant of the second and first centuries B.C. and early first century A.D.

At present it is perhaps a little early to ask that important question, which seems not yet even to have occurred to Christian scholars; and we know that all the pertinent data is not yet assembled and evaluated, for the wily Bedouins * doubtless have still many scroll scraps saved up for bargaining, and will likely find more caves. But it requires no great prophetic gift to foresee a great debate looming in the not-so-distant future over the relative values in Essenism and Christianity. We may yet have a revival of Essenism as a new sect of Christians.

One thing is emerging from the study of the Scrolls—namely, that the beliefs, teachings, and practices of Jesus himself, although not identical in all respects with those of the Essene school that he probably attended during the "silent years," were apparently closer to those of the Essenes than to those of the bishops of the ecumenical council which determined the Nicene Creed of orthodox Christianity. Jesus called himself the Son of Man; they called him the Son of God, the Second Person of the Trinity, Very God of Very God.

It is most doubtful if the Essenes or Jesus himself would have agreed with that.

---

*The young Bedouin, Muhammad ed-Deeb, who found the first scroll-bearing cave, has just issued an affidavit correcting, in several respects, the scientists' stories of his find, which actually occurred in 1945. After sharing with his two fellow goatherds the "rolled leather with scrawling on it because my companions and I needed straps for our sandals," he took his share home, hung it in a skin bag in a corner. It "remained hanging for more than two years" until his uncle took it "to show to a dealer in antiquities at Bethlehem, to see if it might be of any value."

3. Who and What Were the Essenes?

Whenever a citizen overhears two of his fellows discussing such commonly debated current questions as whether or not Jesus—or John the Baptist, or John the Beloved Disciple, or Paul the Apostle—could have been an Essene; or whether the Qumran community whose vast library has now been discovered in the Dead Sea caves was an Essene settlement; or whether even the Christian Church itself may not have been just another of the Essene sects; the listening kibitzer is very apt to ask: "And who, I'd like to know, were the Essenes?"

Thereby the questioner is simply raising again an ancient problem, for the Essenes have been called "the great enigma of Hebrew history." Even the origin of their name is a riddle. Over twenty different answers have been given, varying with the derivation of the word from similar sounding words in Hebrew, Aramaic, Syriac, and the Greek—words which, as one scholar wryly remarks, "have been successively tortured to confess the secret connected with this appellation."

These definitions are important, because their number and variety indicate the profound interest in these mysterious people. Also because the earnest efforts and guesses of many scholars trying to penetrate the cloud of obscurity surrounding them furnish a composite picture, surprisingly accurate in many respects in the light of the sensational discoveries in their long-forgotten haunts. Reviewing the alleged characteristics of the Essenes featured in these scholarly derivations, one recalls the old Hindu fable, well worn but singularly appropriate here, of the six blind men who went to "see" the elephant. The one who seized the tail was sure the beast was like a rope, while the man who got hold of the ear compared the animal to a fan, and so on.

Similarly, the Essenes, depending upon what aspect of their characters, occupations, or even geographical location the scholar deemed most important, have been called The Seers, The Pious, The Silent Ones, The Performers of the Law, The Physicians, The Puritans, The Associates, The Retired Ones, The Brethren, The Servants of God, The Men of Essa, The Stout Ones, The Strong Race, The Mysterious Ones, The Holiness Sect, The Third Sect (after the Sadducees and the Pharisees), The Prophesiers, The Saints, The School of Healers, The Bathers, The Daily Baptists, The Observers of The Laws of Purity, and The Apron-Wearers.

One interesting extra guess was made by the fourth-century Church Father, Epiphanius. After stating that the Essenes were really the Ossenes, or Strong Men, he suggests in another writing that they were properly Jesseans, after either Jesse, the Father of King David, or Jesus. Epiphanius seeks to justify this latter rather startling connection of Essenes, Jesseans, and Jesus by asserting that in Hebrew the name Jesus means a physician, and the Essenes were healers and taught the doctrines Jesus did!

That statement has been looked upon by other scholars for centuries with considerable amusement as a very wild guess, but while it is extremely unlikely that the Essenes were named for the Jesus who was born so long after they were so named, the assertion that he and they were healers and taught the same doctrines must now be recognized as rather close to the truth.

Neither the Bible, Old Testament or New, nor the Talmud mentions the Essenes, a fact which of course pushed them further into the background of anonymity

21

and mystery. There is ample Bible recognition of the Sadducees and Pharisees: the former are mentioned fourteen times, and the latter ninety-eight times, in the New Testament—mostly in the Gospels.

It is possible that the Essenes were sometimes meant when Jesus condemned the Pharisees for their meticulous observance of the fine points of the law, especially their ceremonial washings. True, the Essenes did resemble the Pharisees in their careful keeping of the Law, and could easily have been mistaken for them by those who did not know of the many other ways in which they differed. And it is quite likely that a century or more before the time of Jesus, the Essenes and Pharisees had much more in common when both sects worked together to exalt the Mosaic Law as a protest against other Jews who then were relaxing their loyalty to the Torah under the influence of the Greek ideas.

If, however, anyone is inclined to use the condemnation of the Pharisees by Jesus and his followers as proof that Christianity could not have been derived from or influenced by the Essenes, let it be noted that Paul often boasted of being a Pharisee of the Pharisees. His various letters in the New Testament show both in vocabulary and doctrine that he was familiar with and accepted many of the Essene teachings. He also frequented Antioch, where the disciples of Jesus were first called Messianists or Christians, and Damascus; and these two Syrian cities probably contained colonies or chapters of Essenes, as scholars now studying the Qumran manuscripts are led to suspect.

Besides the Pharisees, Sadducees, and Essenes, the historian Josephus mentions the "Galileans" or Zealots as a fourth Jewish sect or social-religious group. The Zealots were a very nationalistic, direct-action party with "an inviolable attachment to liberty," indifferent to suffering and fearless of death. One of them named Simon is mentioned several times in the New Testament. In fact, he

22

was one of Jesus' original twelve disciples, but this is rather obscured in the King James Version because the English word "zealot" is never used. In Luke 6:15 and Acts 1:13 he is called Simon Zelotes, as if Zelotes were his last name, while in Matthew 10:4 and Mark 3:18 he is Simon the Canaanite, as if he were from the town of Cana. Really, however, the translators erred here, for the Hebrew word "canna" means zealous, just as does the Greek "zelotes." Only in the Acts passage does even the Revised Standard Version frankly call him "Simon the Zealot."

That Jesus had a Zealot among his so-called "Twelve Apostles" was evidently blurred and played down by the Gospel writers and editors. And since the term "Galilean" was almost synonymous with Zealot, and Jesus was twice in Luke (22:59 and 23:6, 7) called a Galilean, and John (4:45) tells how the Galileans welcomed him as one of them, there was at least a "fellow-traveler" implication in the charge before Pilate that Jesus was a Galilean who "stirreth up the people."

For the Zealots were the party on the extreme left of center in Jesus' day. At the far right were the solidly wealthy, conservative Sadducees. The political, social, and religious center was held by the Pharisees of various shades. They themselves were roughly divisible into three groups. On the Pharisee right were the followers of the comparatively conservative Shammai; in the middle were the Hillellites, followers of that liberal teacher Hillel whose grandson Gamaliel was Paul's teacher in Pharisee-ism. Most deviating of the Pharisees were the Apocalyptic Pharisees, a "Modernist" group who laid much stress on such books as Daniel, Ezekiel, and the noncanonical Enoch.

If the Sadducees were on the extreme right, and the Pharisees of all stripes in the center, then going left from them were the Essenes, Gnostics, and Zealots, in that order. The Essenes were hardly to be distinguished from the Apocalyptic Pharisees, for they too used the apocalypses of Daniel, Enoch, Ezekiel, but they went farther and wrote their own books—probably adding sections to Enoch. Socially they deviated even more, forming self-sustaining cooperatives.

The Gnostics were not really a separate party or sect, for they were found, to some extent, in several parties, as individuals and small groups emphasizing Wisdom, Knowledge, and the Word of God as mystic, semipersonal entities. The first part (and several other parts) of John's Gospel—"In the beginning was the Word, and the Word was with God, and the Word was God . . ."—is pure Gnosticism. Gnostic mysticism had come to the Jews from the East, from India and Persia and Babylon; it had appealed to them in their Babylonian captivity, and they had brought much of it back home with them in the Return.

Gnosticism permeated Essene teachings, but the Essenes still held firmly to the Jewish Torah, while the real Gnostics went farther left. But the extreme left, the Zealot party, was anything but Gnostic. They were no theosophic mystics, but fighting radicals, the shock troops and guerrillas of Jewish nationalism, "the Galileans whose blood Pilate had mingled with their sacrifices." (Luke 13:1)

The late scholar, Dr. Ralph Marcus of the University of Chicago, who is so greatly missed in the ranks of those qualified to translate and interpret the Qumran Scrolls, suggested (in the *Journal of Biblical Literature*, Sept. 1954) the following analogies and correspondences between our modern social groups and those of Jesus' day, warning us not to press the parallels too far.

The Sadducees, he remarked, corresponded to the Republicans in the United States, the Shammaite Pharisees to the Conservative Democrats, the Hillellite Pharisees to the New Deal Democrats, the Apocalyptic Pharisees to the Radical Democrats and Progressives, the Essenes to the Socialists, the Gnostics to the group that Theodore Roosevelt called the "lunatic fringe," and the Zealots to the Communists.

While the comparisons are not altogether accurate, they are rather apt, save perhaps that the Gnostics, who were far from lunacy, were probably closer to the socio-political group we call "egg-heads" today.

Not only Paul but Jesus himself probably fitted best into the Essene classification among these seven groups at the beginning of his ministry, whether or not he actually joined that brotherhood as a full-fledged member. He certainly advocated and preached their beliefs to a remarkable extent, as every newly translated Qumran scroll reveals. He differed from them on some points, but the area of agreement was much greater.

One little point of interest in comparing the morality and ethics of Essenes and Christians is the fact that the English Orientalist, Dean Humphrey Prideaux of Norwich, in his popular book, *The Old and New Testament Connected*, (London 1716; part ii, book v) gives a long description of the Essenes based on Philo, Josephus, and Pliny, in which the Dean accuses the Essenes of violating the law of God by their repudiation of slavery "which the holy Scriptures of the New Testament (Philemon 1:9-21), as well as the Old, allow."

Another point: Whatever the results of the future debate on the Scrolls, it should always be remembered that the first "voice of one crying in the wilderness, Prepare ye the way of the Lord, make his paths straight," following Isaiah's suggestion in his beautiful 40th chapter, was not John the Baptist but the great unknown Teacher of Righteousness of the Community of the New Covenant. His "Manual of Discipline" (as Christian scholars have named it but which they themselves apparently called "The Covenant of the Community") bade them to "leave the city of men of iniquity to go into the wilderness to clear the path for HUHA*, as it is written: 'In the wilderness clear the path of HUHA; make level in the desert a highway for our God.'" (Column viii, lines 13-14).

The Essenes of the Qumran community, which was evidently the headquarters for the whole sect, judging by the great size of the library, were trail blazers. It is no wonder that it was hard to account for them. They were somewhat anonymous mystery men because the words and thought forms to describe them had not yet been coined. Certainly, they built on the foundations laid for them by other men, notably the greater of the Hebrew prophets. But they reinterpreted the writings of those prophets in a fresh way, in accord with the "new covenant," or new arrangement of religious ideas, which they believed had been revealed to them through the instructions and interpretations of that great unknown prophet whom they called the Teacher of Righteousness, or Righteous Master.

The book of Isaiah (which was such a favorite of Jesus and of the Qumran Covenanters) changes pace and character abruptly with the beginning of the 40th chapter, so that chapters 40-55 (according to some scholars 40-66) are attributed to Second Isaiah, often called The Great Unknown Prophet of the Exile. Overzealous new admirers of the Qumran Teacher of Righteousness have wished to identify him with this second Isaiah, but the chronology is way off. Yet there is little doubt that this hitherto-unknown figure and still-anonymous personality will eventually take his place with the world's honored pioneers

*This four-letter word (tetragrammaton) HUHA, was a sort of pious subterfuge to avoid the sin of uttering the sacred name YHVH (Yahveh), or Jehovah as it later became when the vowels of another word were combined with the consonants of YHVH. People of many faiths are reluctant to repeat the name of their deity. The present writer knew a dear old Christian lady who would not name Jesus, even in a hymn, but always sang: "Hum-um, Lover of my soul . . ."

of thought and most important organizers of new religions.

When an Essene commentator explains the 2nd verse of the 2nd chapter of the prophecies of Habakkuk as referring to the Teacher of Righteousness, he adds: "who had been taught by God all the secrets of the words of His servants the prophets." Thus the torch of progress in the relay race of mankind is ever passed on from one pioneer to another.

The stature of the great unknown Essene prophet was such that his contemporaries were puzzled to account for him by their own limited knowledge. He had drawn inspiration from many wells, not all of them Jewish. The Essene books reveal a wide range of contacts. The powerful influence of the Persian prophet Zarathustra is very evident in the dualism of the conflict depicted in the Essene library book, The War of the Sons of Light with the Sons of Darkness. Some see traces of Buddhism here and there; and the shades of great classic thinkers, Roman and Greek, especially Alexandrian Greek, hover in the deeper recesses of the mind of the Teacher of Righteousness, who was probably responsible—either directly or through his pupils—for a great deal of the typically Essene literature found in the caves, much of it anonymous.

We may find in this hitherto-unknown pioneer thinker the author of some of the falsely signed (pseudepigraphic) books, the writers of which employed the by-lines of famous men like Enoch, Ezra, Baruch, Moses, Abraham, or Solomon in order to speak what needed to be said and yet avoid the death penalty for presuming to add books to the Hebrew Bible after the canon (official list) had been closed with Ezra. After the third century B.C. any man who assumed the role of prophet—that is, wrote scripture —was, according to Zechariah 13:3, to be thrust through by his own father and mother.

It has long been suspected that the Enochan literature,

as the many books are called that assume the name of
Enoch, the "seventh from Adam," who was translated
into heaven, was written by Essenes. Now, the many copies of Enochan and other pseudepigraphic books found in
the various caves confirm that suspicion. Information
from the scholars identifying and translating the Qumran
manuscript fragments reports eight different Enochan
books from one cave alone, all in Aramaic.

We do not know how many of these many noncanonical scriptures were written by the Teacher of Righteousness and the other men on his faculty and patiently
reproduced in many copies by the scribes in the large
"scriptorium," or publishing house, now excavated. But
the number was very great, to judge by the thousands of
fragments carelessly left by the ignorant native tribesmen
who pillaged the storage grottoes in the past twenty centuries. And when you consider how often the vicinity was
frequented by fanatics of faiths whose leaders would like
nothing better than to see all such damning documents of
heretical and perverse sectaries destroyed, you wonder
that any scrolls or even fragments have remained until
today. Several scholars who have never been accused of
harboring superstitious ideas have stated that it is nothing
less than a miracle that so much of the Essene library still
exists.

Let us take up the Qumran Essene commentary on the
Old Testament book of the Prophet Habakkuk, a book beloved by orthodox Christians and much quoted for such
verses as: "Woe unto him that giveth his neighbor
drink. . . ." "Oh Lord, revive thy work in the midst of the
years . . . in wrath remember mercy," and, of course, the
famous verse: " . . . but the just shall live by his faith."

The Book of Habakkuk in our Bibles is short enough—
only three chapters—but the Essene commentator, who
quotes verse after verse of that book, explaining each
verse as he proceeds, stops at the end of the second chap-

28

ter, as if that were the end of the book and he had never heard of a third chapter.

Uninformed but loyal defenders of the three-chapter Habakkuk in the King James Bible have countered with the argument that the third chapter of the Essene commentary was torn or broken off the outside of the leather scroll. To the contrary, however, it is the beginning of the book, parts of columns one and two, where the commentator discusses the first four verses of chapter one of Habakkuk, that is partly worn off the outside of the scroll.

The end of the scroll was rolled inside, and the text ends with the comment on the beautiful last verse of chapter two, which stands alone in four lines of writing at the top of an otherwise blank column, followed by another totally blank column. In contrast, back in column six of the manuscript, the second chapter follows immediately after the end of the first chapter, without even a space left between.

Because this Essene commentary on Habakkuk, found in the first-opened Dead Sea cave along with a much older copy of Isaiah, shows by internal evidence that it was written as late as about 65 B.C. and perhaps a little later, we are justified in presuming that the third chapter must have been added at some time after that date. An editor simply attached it to the "Book of the Prophecies of Habakkuk," evidently lifting these nineteen verses from a collection of psalms where one was entitled "A Prayer of Habakkuk." That editor was rather clumsy. In making the third chapter, he appropriated two psalms (one now found in Habakkuk 3:1-16, and the second in 3:17-19a) and even included the musical notation, "To the director of stringed instruments," which he found at the beginning of a third psalm and which now appears awkwardly (3:19b) as the closing phrase of Habakkuk's important prophecies, instead of using the very beautiful original ending of the book (Habakkuk 2:20). The original ending was the verse that millions of Christians today repeat

at the opening of worship in their churches: ". . . the Lord
is in his holy temple: let all the earth keep silence before
him."

But it is not only the little Book of Habakkuk that
has been altered from the form in which the author left
it. The "historical" Books of First and Second Samuel will
need radical changes in several large sections where the
older versions in the manuscripts of the Essene library
(found in Qumran Cave 4, plus additional parts pur-
chased afterwards from the Arabs) make much better
sense than the ones on which the King James and all the
revised versions were based.

Most of the super-orthodox will refuse to believe that
anything can be improved in "Mother's Bible," and many
good Christians will quote the verses in the last chapter
of "Revelation" as the Johannine apocalypse at the end
of the New Testament is popularly called, verses 18b and
19 in chapter 22:

". . . If any man shall add unto these things, God shall
add unto him the plagues that are written in this book:
And if any man shall take away from the words of the
book of this prophecy, God shall take away his part out
of the book of life, and out of the holy city, and from
the things which are written in this book."

This warning or threat was fairly common in Jewish
books in one form or another. In the next to the last
(perhaps originally the last) chapter (104th) of the Book
of Enoch, the patriarch advises: ". . . do not change or
abridge anything of my words, but write them all down
truthfully." And in the Old Testament Book of Deuteronomy, chapter 4, verse 2, in anticipation of the giving
of the Ten Commandments in Chapter 5, the Lord commands:

"Ye shall not add unto the word which I command you,
neither shall ye diminish ought from it. . . ."

But Jesus apparently disregarded this injunction, for, according to the first three Gospels, when approached by the Rich Young Ruler, Jesus recited only five of the Ten Commandments as important, and Mark (10:19) has him adding a new one: "Do not defraud."

By "this book" at the end of the Johannine apocalypse, it is commonly supposed the entire Bible is meant—most Christians not yet being aware that the rest of the Bible was long in circulation before the very doubtful Apocalypse of John was finally added. There was an Apocalypse of Peter which was preferred in Rome and the Apocalypse of Enoch, a favorite in the East. But Apocalypses were going out of style, and only one could be permitted, if any. Peter's and Enoch's were dropped. Finally, reluctantly, and at the end of the Bible, John's was let in. Personally, I like the book and consider it colorful and splendid in its symbolic imagery. Even the threatening verses in the last chapter have the quaint charm of the line on many an old tombstone: "Cursed be he who moves my bones!"

As we have noted, democracy in religion or religious monasticism was virtually unknown in the Mediterranean world of the day. But such groups of monks were common in India long before the Christian era. It is possible that the founders of the Essene sect had heard through Greek or Persian sources about the groups of democratic monks encountered in the east by the surprised soldiers of Alexander the Great.

Extreme national consciousness of the Jewish people, plus the strong belief in the divinity of anointed kings, even after the Hebrew monarchy had long fallen, led the Jews to expect the coming of a Messianic ruler who would restore the kingship and its autocratic power. They had, as well, firm faith in a priestly aristocracy. Thus completely conditioned, the nation looked askance on a religious brotherhood that was democratic, self-governing, that even elected its officers by the votes of all its members, and that crowned its heresy by refusing to participate in the animal sacrifice system of the Temple at nearby Jerusalem!

More surprising still, the Essenes' novel approach to religion was linked into an equally revolutionary social set-up. It was really a new form of social order, an ideal cooperative commonwealth in miniature, which the leaders of the Essenes established, perhaps first in small groups in or near towns where they would be tolerated, and later centering in larger self-contained colonies in the valleys and gorges leading from the hills round about Jerusalem down through the limestone cliffs to the great salt lake now called the Dead Sea. One of these larger and earlier Essene centers was probably at En-Gedi, "the Spring of the Kid," the place in the Judean wilderness where David hid from Saul in a great cave "among the rocks of the wild goats." This very cave, a huge one where Bar-Coch-ba* is said to have hid his army, was rediscovered in the widespread hunt for manuscripts sparked by the discoveries in the caves further north near the other and chief Essene community center at the Wady (Valley of) Qumran.

Doubtlessly, the new social organization of these Essene centers was due to the recognized failure of the old monarchy, both before and after the Hasmonean rulers, and to the corruption of the Temple priests. Thus, the Essenes had a chance to try out their fine new idea of a cooperative communitarian brotherhood and an irreproachable priesthood like that of the old Zadokite priests established by Solomon.

---

*A Jewish military Messiah who lived a century after Jesus.

4. Contemporary Views of the
Desert Sect

Josephus (A.D. 37-95) was much impressed with the economic system of the Essenes, pointing out that:

"They despise wealth, and their socialism is remarkable. None among them can be found richer than another. It is their law that all who enter the sect must divide their property among the members of the society, with the result that there is never seen among them either abject poverty nor great wealth, for, since every man's possessions are put into the common treasury, they all have, like brothers, one inheritance."

Philo (? B.C.—A.D. 50) saw deeper into the communitarian set-up and understood its productivity of dividends in friendship and fellowship as well as its economic advantages. He is much more enthusiastic and appreciative. The following excerpts are from his book, *Apology for the Jews*, a work lost long ago but happily preserved in part in quotations by the church historian Eusebius (A.D. 264-349) in his book, *Preparation for the Gospel*:

"Our Lawgiver [Philo thought of Moses, not knowing then of the Teacher of Righteousness] trained in community living thousands of disciples called Essenes, probably because of their holiness. They live in large societies located in many Judean cities and villages.

"Their organization is not based on family kinship, in which a man has no choice, but on zeal for virtue and love

33

of all men . . . They enjoy the only genuine liberty, as is proved by their way of life. None of them is striving to get possession of any private property . . . or anything to get rich by, for everything is put into the common pool, which supplies the wants of all alike.

"Dwelling together in one place, they therefore study together, eat together and associate with one another, expending all their energies for the common good. There is division of labor, different men to different kinds of work, but whatever may be their work, they do it with vigor, patience, and good cheer, never excusing themselves from labor on account of cold, heat, or changes of weather. They are at work before sunrise and after the sun has set, considering their work to be the best sort of gymnastic exercise, pleasanter and of more advantage than mere athletics."

Then Philo explains more in detail the daily life in the Qumran monastic community, giving a vivid picture of great interest now that the nearly completed excavations of the last six years have brought to light the very rooms where these men congregated, the gardens they cultivated, the pottery, forge, and bakery where they worked, the scriptorium where they made copies of their sacred books, the dishes they used in their sacramental meals, the pools where they bathed and perhaps were baptized, and over a thousand graves in the adjacent cemetery where their bones now lie:

"Those experienced in agriculture till the soil; those understanding animals tend the flocks; those skilled in husbandry care for the swarms of bees. Artisans and craftsmen of all kinds anticipate the need of their manufactured products. In fact, every genuine need of life is provided for and no necessity overlooked. . . .

"They eat at the same table and are satisfied with a simple diet, regularly repeated, loving frugal fare and abhorring luxury as a disease of mind and body. They have common raiment as well, for in winter thick cloaks are ready and in summer cheap sleeveless tunics in store to which each man can go and take his pick, for what belongs to one is the property of all, and what belongs to all is the property of each.

"If any man falls sick, whatever medical treatment or resources are available are devoted to his cure, and his care and recovery are the concern of the whole community. Old men, though they may be childless, are thus assured of happiness and tender care in their old age, just as if they were the fathers of children both numerous and affectionate. Even more, they are honored and cared for from the free good will of the many, rather than from the bounden duty of blood-relatives. . . .

"So enviable, then, is the Essene way of life, that not only private citizens, but also mighty kings are filled with amazement and admiration at them, and have honored the fraternity by lavishing praise and honor upon these respected and venerated men."

Josephus, who spent three years either in the Qumran community center or nearby, and had opportunities for closer observation than did Philo, gives the daily program as followed by Essenes, a routine with several items of interest to students of comparative religion, particularly when amplified by additions recently made available by the discovery and translation of the Qumran cave manuscripts. Josephus wrote:

"So peculiarly pious are they that they never mention secular affairs before the sun rises, but utter certain ancestral prayers, as if entreating it to rise. Then they are dismissed by the overseers to the tasks in which they are skilled, where they work hard until the fifth hour (about 11 a.m.), when they once more assemble, put on linen aprons, and bathe in cold water. After this rite of purification, they retire to a private room from which strangers are excluded, and enter, fully purified, into their dining-room as if it were a sacred temple, and quietly take their seats.

"The baker then places a loaf of bread before each in turn, and the cook gives each a plate of one kind of food.

But no one may taste it until a priest says grace, and after they have breakfasted, he returns thanks, for both before and after eating they praise God the giver of life.

"Then they lay aside their white sacred garments, and go back to work until evening, when they return to eat supper together and with any visiting strangers. No noise or uproar is ever allowed to profane the house, for whoever speaks must do so in turn. To outsiders, the silence seems strange and mysterious to explain, but it is due to their sobriety, which is the result of the fact that they are all given just enough food and drink to satisfy their needs, but no more."

Pliny, a Latin writer contemporary (A.D. 23-79) with both Philo and Josephus, mentions the Essenes briefly, just after he has described the Dead Sea, saying:

"On the West Side [of the sea] and far enough away to escape its noxious fumes, are the Hessenes, a race by themselves and remarkably different from all other men in the whole wide world. They live without women,* having renounced all sexual love. They live without money, and for companionship they have palm trees! Their ranks are continually recruited from the numbers of people who, weary from struggling with adverse fortune, resort to this way of living. So, strange to say, without any births among them, this race has lasted for thousands of ages, because so fruitful for them is the life-weariness of others!"

Pliny's estimate of the length of the existence of the sect apparently stems more from his enthusiasm than his knowledge, but his fervor tinged with surprise at there being such a unique race on earth is matched by Philo in his *Every Virtuous Man Is Free* in which, although he does not mention them by name, the Essenes are plainly meant:

*Apparently, Pliny was wrong in this statement. For early in the exhumation of the 1200 graves of the Qumran cemetery, the skeletons of at least six women were found.

"There are still God-guided men today who live naturally and reasonably, men who are themselves so free that they

inspire their neighbors also with the spirit of freedom. There are not many of them, it is true, but that is not to be wondered at, for high nobility of that degree is always rare. These men have attained to it by separating themselves from the common crowd that they may dedicate their lives to the study of the great truths of nature. . . ."

And he adds the ringing challenge to them which we've quoted in Chapter 2, the call for them to come forth and preach, which brings us to the present consideration of the teachings of the Essenes and the preaching of Jesus, and the connection between them.

5. Light on the Education of Jesus

Again we wonder: Was Jesus a young member of the Essene brotherhood at the time Philo's treatise, *Every Virtuous Man Is Free*, was written? Of course it was in Greek and was probably available sooner or later in the large Essene library at Qumran, especially because it contained so long an account of Essene theory and practice.

Philo was a native of Alexandria, Egypt, and spent most of his life there; and, near that great city, second itself only to Rome, there was then another Essene community on the shores of Lake Mareotis. Philo wrote about them, too, in another of his books, *Concerning the Contemplative Life*, including them in that particular treatise because he deemed them more contemplative than the Essenes in Palestine, whom he thought more practical.

The Alexandrian branch was called the Therapeutae, but they were not physicians or attendants or healers, as the name might imply; it was a heavenly therapy they sought for themselves as they waited upon God in prayer and meditation. They differed in some ways from the Essenes by the Dead Sea, for they were known to include women, they fasted, they did not prophesy, they were strict vegetarians, and they were not communitarian, each one having his own hut a short distance from the rest; nor did they put all their money in a common fund.

But they were typically Essenian in their renunciation of money, in frugality of living, their combining of plain living and high thinking, their mysticism, their interest in hymns and hymn composition, their sunrise worship, their repudiation of animal sacrifices, their asceticism, their connection with Eastern (Persian or Hindu) mystic contemplation, their basic Judaism, their obvious Gnostic coloring, and their studious love of books—especially the Enochan literature and similar "secret" writings having to do with the calendar, sacred numbers, apocalypses, and wisdom books.

It was not a long journey between Alexandria and Jerusalem, and was particularly cheap and pleasant by sea, so it is very likely that the two Essene communities exchanged books and visits. By this line of communication, Philo's books could easily have come into the hands of Jesus in Palestine, whether he was in an Essene community there or not. The translation from Alexandrian Greek into Aramaic of Philo's works and those of other Greek writers would not have been difficult for the learned Essene scholars of the library and scriptorium of the Qumran community center. And the reverse process took place a little later, when the Aramaic originals of the early Christian records, writings, and anthologies were gradually collated, compiled, edited, and translated into what is now known as "the original Greek" of the Christian New Testament. Such scholarly work may actually have been started there and been transferred elsewhere when the Roman Tenth Legion approached and began the destruction of Jerusalem and neighboring Jewish settlements about A.D. 68.

But the translation of Philo's Every Virtuous Man Is Free and Concerning the Contemplative Life from the Greek into Aramaic for Jesus' information was probably not as necessary as we should have thought a few years ago. The widely circulated and believed picture of Jesus as an uneducated and unlearned artisan, a sort of journeyman carpenter, whose wisdom and uncanny understanding was a very special gift of God from on high (enabling him even at the age of twelve to confound and out-argue in the Temple the most learned elder scholars of the Jewish race) is fading rapidly. It is too much like a hill-billy preacher who never finished grammar school standing up in a pulpit, opening the Bible at random, and, by sheer God-given inspiration, preaching a wonderful soul-saving sermon "by the power of the Holy Spirit" which converts even the atheistic professors who drop in out of curiosity.

That crude conception of Jesus should have been erased long ago, for there was evidence enough to disprove it, but it is absolutely inadmissible today in the light of recent linguistic studies in the Koine (pronounced koy-nay), the mixture of various languages—mostly Greek—that resulted from Alexander the Great's conquest of the then-known world. The Koine was, as the name means in both Greek and Koine, the common or universal language of the time, a sort of Esperanto used in conversation, in commerce, and in writing for the "mass market" during the centuries immediately before and after A.D. 1, until Latin gradually took its place as the lingua franca of the Mediterranean world.

The so-called Greek New Testament was written not in the classical or literary Greek but in the ordinary Koine. That this fact was not realized until the 20th century is certainly one of the worst mistakes of scholarship, and with tragic effects, which I'd like to go into here as pertinent to our exposition.

Training of young men for the Christian ministry included for several centuries (and does yet in some places) a long and painful experience, learning Greek, which meant learning classical Greek first. After a year or more wrestling with "Elementary Greek," during which time the boy was supposed to familiarize himself with the extremely complicated cases, genders, numbers, voices, tenses, moods, conjugations, declensions, and other inflections of the most inflected language ever developed by mankind, he was led on by "easy" stages until he got into Homer, when he found that in order to read Greek poetry, he had to learn a whole new set of inflections. If his courage survived Homer, he might be permitted to read Herodotus and Thucydides for "Historical Greek," and then Sophocles, Aeschylus, and Aristophanes for "Greek Drama."

These various kinds of classical Greek usually required the seven or eight years of high school and college, and the student was in the first year of theological seminary before he began what they called "New Testament Greek," which the professor implied would be pretty rough going. It was, he admitted apologetically, "not very good Greek, a sort of degenerate dialect." We found it very smooth going, however, and revelled in its tangy phrases and rich idioms, and felt more at home in it than in any of the classical varieties, perhaps because we were Americans and accustomed to picturesque, democratic language.

The tragic effects of this "course of sprouts" were two-fold. First, over half the young men who had started to study for the ministry dropped out, mostly because of the Greek, although alleging other reasons. Second, after such a tough time with Greek, we were firmly convinced that the professors were undoubtedly correct when they told us that Jesus, since he had been brought up in a Jewish home in Palestine, probably spoke Aramaic, the Hebrew dialect then in use there, and never learned Greek. So his sayings and teaching had to be translated by the Gospel writers from Aramaic into Greek, as we now find them in the New Testament. Incidentally, we were sure that an uneducated young Jewish carpenter wouldn't learn Greek, going through what we had endured, unless he had to.

We didn't know then, nor did the professors themselves suspect that Jesus probably learned the Koine the same way we had learned English, by hearing it spoken all around him. When I later got into Hebrew and Aramaic myself, I decided Greek was comparatively easy.

The myth of Jesus' ignorance of Greek, at least of the Koine, should be completely exploded by the contents of the Qumran caves. The evidence accumulating from the finds there indicates that we must hereafter have more respect for the accuracy and trustworthiness of the Septuagint, the so-called Greek Old Testament, which was written in the Koine, as is now rather tardily admitted. When I was a boy, studying my Sunday School lessons, I noted that when the New Testament quoted the Old—when Matthew wrote: "As it was spoken by Jeremy (or Elias, or Esaias) the prophet," —the quotation Matthew gave wasn't correct according to the Old Testament passage he was supposed to be quoting. Why didn't he have it absolutely the same? Didn't he have his Bible in front of him? And he didn't even spell their names right: they should be Jeremiah, Elijah, and Isaiah. I had to go to college and seminary to find the answers.

The answers to such questions and many others which even a child can and should ask about the Bible are to be found in certain scientific facts, long hidden, some formerly unknown, others purposely either concealed, or "played down" by paternal theologians. Such is the fact that the Koine Septuagint was the Bible of Jesus, of the Gospel writers, of Paul, and of Apollos, who was a first century A.D. Christian missionary, and of the earliest Church Fathers.

And the Scrolls from the Salty Sea caves fit right into the emerging new pattern restoring the Man Jesus to the world, the Great Teacher who learned from the Hebrew prophets, from the Essene teachers, from the great thinkers of the Greek Alexandrian culture of his time. He thought it all over and created his own message from the best of all he had studied, and finally dramatized it as the Suffering Servant Savior Son of Man, who was also Teacher of Righteousness and the Messiah of the coming great millenial Kingdom of Righteousness and Peace, to be ushered in when the Prince of Peace should lead the Sons of Light to victory at Armageddon over the Sons of Darkness.

There have been scholars of recent years, writing long before the Qumran Essene library was unearthed, who have come to the conclusion that Jesus was not the unlettered rustic artisan who "spake as man never spake" simply because he was "filled with the Holy Spirit" and God used him as a mouthpiece.

Dr. Thomas Walker, in *What Jesus Read* (Scribners, 1925), calls him "a well read working man of his time, whose own message was in no small measure due to the fact that he had enriched his mind by a careful perusal of the work of all types of sincere seekers after the truth of God . . . not only in the officially sacred books, but also in the many other religious books and tracts which were circulating in his day." What those "other religious books" were in which Jesus "searched the scripture," Dr. Walker further specifies as those with which "he became acquainted . . . through the library of some private circle or circles . . . types of literature such as are now represented by a few extra-canonical books which have fortunately survived the ravages of time."

In *The Literary Background of the New Testament*, (Macmillan, 1928), page 13, George Hurst states that for this well read young Nazarene's literary appetite "ample provision existed," and that "Jesus could ransack some of the chief depositories of religious books in Galilee. Those repositories were in the private houses of well-to-do people, in the meeting places of various religious circles or sects whose books were held in common, as well as in the synagogues."

Such religious groups, meeting privately and circulating books of a particular type among themselves, appear to have been common in the time of Jesus. Particularly so in "Galilee of the Gentiles," which apparently was culturally broadened by the busy stream of traffic that ran through it, back and forth between Alexandria and Athens from the west and Damascus and other cities of the Decapolis. These were ten Graeco-Roman cities in Syria, mostly east and south of the Sea of Galilee. The Gospels refer to several visits by Jesus in the Decapolis itself, and there is no doubt that he was not only aware of but influenced by these nearby centers of culture and their neighborhood echoes.

It is significant also that the period during which the "Ten Cities" flourished (1st and 2nd centuries B.C. and 1st century A.D.) was coincident with the heyday of the nearby Essenes.

Dr. J. E. H. Thomson, in his *Books Which Influenced Our Lord and His Apostles* (1891), contemplates Jesus hurrying, after work, to some place where Essenes lived and there reading avidly till after midnight the Enochan books with their apocalyptic visions of the Son of Man and the blessed days of the Messianic Kingdom to come.

These anticipations or foregleams in books like Thomson's unconsciously heralding the present-day discovery of Jesus' intimate relationship with the Essenes were bound to occur in the writings of the more observant and conscientious scholars. The similarities between Christian and Essene teachings were too obvious to be overlooked. That these authors did not go further and jump to the conclusion which now seems equally obvious to us was probably due to their long conditioning in a theological atmosphere and pious circles where the idea of Christianity before Christ, or even a pre-Christian Jewish ethical system equal to the Sermon on the Mount, was simply unthinkable.

Yet the recognition of the estimable qualities of the Essenes and their strange resemblance to Christians in at least a few respects did creep into certain books a half-century and more ago. The same year (1891) that Dr. Thomson dared suggest that Jesus may have sat up nights reading the noncanonical Enoch, the great Cambridge scholar, Dr. F. J. Foakes-Jackson, wrote his classic *History of the Christian Church to A.D. 461*. In it he made what was then considered a dangerously radical admission, stating:

"The object of the Sadducee was to conform himself to the world, that of the Pharisee to live in, yet separated from it; but the Essene introduced a new principle destined to have a very powerful influence on the subsequent development of Christianity. His idea was to form a kingdom of God isolated from the world. He withdrew himself from all that was profane in order to be nearer to God. The Essene communities were distinguished, partly by an excess of Pharisaism, a morbid craving after moral purity, and partly by an admixture of foreign customs borrowed from the religions of the East."

Dr. Foakes-Jackson wisely refrained from specifying what these borrowings from the East were, although he must have known, even then, that those customs (and ideas) included many that became very important in the early Christian communities.

But Dr. Foakes-Jackson's temporary spirit of scientific objectivity, which led him to admit on page 12 that the Jewish Essenes had introduced a new principle that powerfully influenced Christianity, forsook him on page 14 as he approached the end of his chapter, and he became again the partisan apologist, piously playing it safe with:

"The history of Christianity shows how all that was best in Judaism together with far nobler truths than Israel had known were presented to the world."

What those "far nobler truths" were, or are, is becoming increasingly difficult to specify, as translations of Jewish books of the century before and the century after the birth of Jesus become available.

So, to the teachings of Hillel (75 B.C.-A.D. 10), whose

45

famous "loving-kindness to all" reflected the "sweetness and light" of his own personality, and who taught his followers: "Do not unto others that which is hateful unto thee" (a generation before Jesus restated it in positive terms), and the similar doctrines of Hillel's grandson and disciple, Gamaliel, at whose feet Paul was proud to have learned the Torah, we now are able to add the fine psalms, prayers, maxims, and doctrines of the Dead Sea Scrolls.

Surely with the evidence at hand, any fair-minded Christian should admit that Jesus was not a miraculous incarnation of a Son of God, pre-existent in the heavens and sent to earth as the long-awaited Messiah, to suffer and die on the cross for the sins of Adam and all Adam's children as an atonement to appease the wrath of his own Father-God, even if the Nazarene himself may have had some such idea toward the end. Rather, the personality of Jesus was the remarkable but natural product, outgrowth, flowering, and fruiting of the living, thinking, suffering, and teaching of many generations of Hebrew prophets and law-givers, priests and students, religious leaders and ethical teachers.

And, by the same token, surely now any fair-minded Jew, knowing that his people all along have refused to accept the doctrine of Jesus' alleged miraculous birth of a virgin mother and his resurrection bodily from the grave, and have been shocked at the mere suggestion that God could beget a son, should at least recognize Jesus as one of the great prophets of his own race—a prophet misunderstood and without honor heretofore in his own country, but of the true line of Jewish progressive religious leaders.

As a matter of fact, and to be hailed with joy by both groups, there has existed for some time now this spirit of friendly rapprochement toward Christianity on the part of the more liberal Jewish rabbis and professors. And these friendly rabbis have been welcomed for some years now in certain Christian churches of liberal persuasions, in churches led by ministers who themselves have been speaking in synagogues and temples led by liberal rabbis.

Unfortunately, the more orthodox Christian leaders refuse to admit that the manuscripts from the Qumran caves are extremely important and will make necessary not only the revision of most of the books of the Bible but also the re-writing of the history of Christian origins. And they oppose the reconsideration and restating of cardinal Christian theological dogmas, if not the abandoning of such doctrines as the special inspiration of canonical Scripture, the incarnation, the virgin birth, the bodily resurrection, and the transubstantiation miracle in the eucharist.

Similarly, but not often so publicly, the more orthodox Jewish rabbis and scholars have been very reluctant to admit even the pre-Christian date of the Scrolls, agreed upon by other Jewish and the great majority of Gentile scholars and substantiated by all sorts of scientific tests— archeological, paleographic, numismatic, and carbon 14 radiation. Furthermore, for an orthodox Jewish student to be asked to doubt the inviolate sacred Masoretic text of his Bible, and especially to accept corrections from allegedly older manuscripts which agree with the Septuagint text as against the Masoretic, is to invite a scornful glance and eloquent shrug of the shoulders at such nonsense. He considers the Alexandrian Septuagint text a blasphemous perversion of the Word of God, full of Christian interpolations, ignorant if not malicious.

Nevertheless and notwithstanding the opposition from the orthodox in both camps and the long years of argument before us, we should remind ourselves, in the words of one of the apocryphal books (I Esdras 4:35), that "Great is truth, and stronger than all things." It will eventually prevail.

The Christian scholars who in the early days of Christianity kept the Jewish Scriptures as an integral part of the growing body of accepted Christian writings, and persisted in keeping the Old Testament with the New Testament, were wise to do so, for the two sections of Revelation belong together. Probably the earliest scholars who recognized this fact had greater difficulty in getting the Jewish Christians to add the Epistles of Paul and the Four Gospels to their own Bible (the Law, the Prophets, and the other writings) than did the latest scholars in persuading the Gentile Christians to retain the old Jewish scriptures.

Very likely, the placing of Matthew's Gospel as the first book in the New Testament (although the compilers must have known that Mark's Gospel was written before either Matthew's or Luke's, since they both obviously quote from Mark's book), was due to Matthew's frequent attempts to show that many of the important events in the life of Jesus were predicted long before by the prophets in Israel. "This was done that it might be fulfilled which was spoken by the prophet" is the formula repeatedly used by Matthew to link the Christian gospel, the New Covenant or Testament, with the Jewish Law and prophets of their Old Covenant. From the modern point-of-view, he often stretched his logic very thin in order to make his point, but his comparisons and references have "got by" for a great many years now, with a few assists occasionally by pious preachers and commentators well trained in semantic casuistry.

6. Sacred Books Omitted from the Bible

Emphasis on the relation between the Old and New Testaments has been even more necessary, and increasingly so, in the centuries since Matthew wrote or compiled his missionary tract. Today, and for many years now, the scriptural but noncanonical books called "apocryphal" by Protestants have been deliberately left out of their Bible.

Surprisingly, this was not officially done. They used to be included between the Old and New Testaments in fine print, and preachers explained that they were not "real Bible," that is, not inspired like the rest of the books, but might be read for historical information and general edification, provided no doctrines of Christian theology were based on them.

The word "apocryphal," which originally meant merely "hidden" (note our word "cryptic" from the same Greek root), came in time to connote something spurious, counterfeit, and untrustworthy. These fourteen apocryphal books of the Jews, although apparently much like the other books, were segregated into a sort of fine-print ghetto between the respectable Jews of the Old Testament and the not only respectable but also very special Christians of the New. No reason for it was given—at least, no understandable one. So the idea naturally prevailed that these books about the Maccabee brothers, and Susanna, Esther, Judith, Esdras, Baruch, Tobit and Manasses, and the wise sayings of Solomon and Jesus the Son of Sirach, were tabu, and not to be read.

49

In my own home, the apocryphal books were in our big old family Bible, although I hunted in vain for them in the little Bibles we used in Sunday School. Looking at the pictures in the "Big Bible" was a permitted occupation on a rainy Sunday afternoon, but Mother always warned me not to go reading that fine-print stuff between Malachi and Matthew.

"Why not?"

"Because it'll spoil your eyes, and you'll need your eyes for studying to be a minister."

Personally, I always read fine print very carefully. And my freedom from the fine-type phobia is doubtless due to my disobedience of Mother's command, for I had no guilty feeling when I read and reread the prohibited apocryphal books.

Of course, I didn't know then that there were other books current in Jesus' day, quoted by him and Paul, which did not even "make" the Apocrypha. To Jesus and his contemporaries these pseudepigraphical books were Holy Scripture. Jude (or whoever was the author of that one-chapter epistle in the New Testament) quotes one of them, The Assumption of Moses, without naming it, when referring to the dispute of Michael the archangel with Satan over the body of Moses. The author of Jude also quotes The Book of Enoch by name as revealing the word of God—that is, as inspired Scripture.

That bold stroke nearly got Jude's letter itself thrown out of the canonical Bible as "guilty by association," contaminated by its mere approving mention of a book not officially recognized!

Enoch was not a mere book but a literature including many books, how many we do not yet know, but it was excluded from both the Christian and Jewish canons. Although a favorite of both Jesus and Paul, copies were apparently destroyed wherever found, and it became known as "The Lost Book of Enoch." But, like the fabled Phoenix which Enoch mentions, it rose from its ashes. In the eighteenth century copies were found in Ethiopia, but they were written in a dead language, and even when translated got very little notice, save among Orientalists and theologians.

Now, however, as I have learned by "grapevine," for scholar-discoverers are naturally very reticent until they get their own books well started, one of the Qumran caves is revealed au monde savant (to scholarly circles) to have contained, along with other pseudepigraphic books, precious fragments of no less than eight different manuscripts, in the original Aramaic, of the "lost" or rather, suppressed Book of Enoch, some of them containing sections not found in the aforesaid Ethiopic Geez manuscripts, which date many centuries later.

I knew there must be copies of Enoch among the manuscripts in those caves after I heard that many unidentified non-Biblical fragments had been found, taken from Cave 4 in September 1952, but my inquiries had received only evasive answers.

The reason these Enoch manuscripts are so terribly important is the fact that their having been found in the Qumran community library definitely dates them and proves many crucial points about Jesus and early Christianity that some of us have long suspected. These points I shall now set forth.

It should first be stated, however, that the find of eight Enochs in these caves of the Essenes, plus the fact that Jews and Christians destroyed all other copies they could get their hands on, may be the clue to the expunging of every reference to the Essenes from the New Testament and to the elimination of Enoch from the canons. When the official canons and doctrines of Jew and Christian were established, in a period when each side hated the other bitterly, as the contemporary literatures of both show historically, then neither side wanted any evidence left around which would reveal that the Essene Book of Enoch was the missing link between Judaism and Christianity! It showed both sides up in the pitiless light of parallelism.

Once the fact is recognized, startling deductions may and indeed must be drawn. For one thing, *Enoch* must go back in the Bible!

Since fragments of Enochan books have been found in at least two other caves besides Cave 4 (which, according to J. T. Milik in the January 1956 issue of the scholarly French quarterly, *Revue Biblique*, contained parts of eight Enochan manuscripts), it is now plain that the Enochan literature played an important role in the literary and religious background of the Essene community.

Whether or not we are justified in assuming that Enoch was used in any fashion similar to what we now call textbooks we do not yet know, but the finding of so many copies already would seem to indicate that it was at least often consulted as a reference book.

If a number of copies of Enoch were in the Qumran community library, and if Jesus spent part of the so-called "silent years" as a member, or associate member, or even only as a resident student, that might explain why he and his disciples were so well acquainted with the Enochan literature that we find not merely the same ideas and doctrines in the New Testament, but even the same phrases and sentences.

These similarities in ideas and vocabulary have been attributed by the orthodox scholars and clergy to interpolations made by overzealous Christians in the Apostolic and later ages. And some have gone so far as to date all Enochan books as Christian—indeed they have explained the quotation from Enoch in Jude's epistle by questioning Jude's right to be in the Bible at all, or by dating it later than the other New Testament books.

But very few people today have ever heard of the Essene *Books of Enoch* because of their suppression by both Christians and Jews in the early centuries.

This peculiar prejudice against the missing-link literature like the Enochan books has persisted in spite of the growing recognition of its importance by more liberal scholars. As long ago as 1914, Dr. R. H. Charles, then Canon of Westminster and the greatest authority on the interbiblical literature, in his book *Religious Development Between the Old and the New Testaments*, writes of the Apocrypha and Pseudepigrapha. He said (page 115) they were composed "between 180 B.C. and A.D. 100," and then went on to say:

"These centuries, especially the two preceding the Christian era, were till recently regarded as the centuries of silence, during which no fresh voice or teaching of God reached the nation. There could hardly be a more mistaken idea. So far from being ages of spiritual stagnation and darkness, they might with justice be described as the two most fruitful centuries in religious life and thought in the history of Israel. No New Testament scholar can understand the New Testament as the culmination of the spiritual development of the past apart from this literature, nor can the Jew explain how Talmudic Judaism came to possess its higher conceptions of the future life, unless he studies this literature as the sequel of the Old Testament."

These words of Canon Charles were almost heretical when he first stated them, but in the forty-odd years since, they have often been quoted in textbooks for students of the apocryphal books. Occasionally, Dr. Charles' book was used in advanced or adult classes in the more liberal Christian church schools.

But the emphasis of these Sunday School studies has been more on the apocryphal books—the First and Second Books of Maccabees, Tobit, Judith, First and Second Esdras, Ecclesiasticus, The Wisdom of Solomon, and several smaller books purporting to be additions to Old Testament books.

One reason why the pseudepigraphical books, which were the ones Dr. Charles particularly meant, were not studied more was the simple fact that they were not available. The only book containing them all was the second volume of Dr. Charles' huge two-volume edition, published in 1913 by the Oxford Press, which had to be imported from England. Very few American clergymen ever saw the book, except perchance in theological seminary libraries. It was too expensive for ministers to buy. I remember how I had to scrimp and save many years ago to buy my copy.

What are these pseudepigraphical books?

They are the real "Dead Sea Scrolls." Some of them we have had before, discovered comparatively recently in Ethiopic, Slavonic, Arabic, Syriac, Greek, Latin, and Armenian translations, but known only to scholars and available in good English renderings only lately—and in costly, seldom-seen books.

But in these discoveries in the caves, we have in the original language some of the books we had before only in comparatively late copies of copies in other tongues. For instance, heretofore most of our manuscripts of the various Enochan books have been Ethiopic sixteenth to eighteenth century A.D. We have one section, commonly called Slavonic or Second Enoch, in Slavonic manuscripts from the fourteenth to seventeenth centuries A.D. (there are a few chapters in Greek and a few verses in Latin). But the eight manuscripts of Enoch found in Cave 4 of the Essene library are in Aramaic, dating from before the time of Jesus!

The same is true of other pseudepigraphic books. Included in Dr. Charles' second volume are the following, in six classifications:

REWRITTEN PRIMITIVE HISTORY
>The Book of Jubilees (109-105 B.C.)

SACRED LEGENDS
>The Epistles of Aristeas (130 B.C.-A.D.?)
>Books of Adam and Eve (A.D. 60-300)

Martyrdom of Isaiah (1st century A.D.)

APOCALYPSES

First Enoch (170-64 B.C.)
Testaments of the Twelve Patriarchs (109-107 B.C.)
Sibylline Oracles (A.D. 80)
Assumption of Moses (A.D. 7-30)
Second Enoch (A.D. 1-50)
Second Baruch (A.D. 50-100)
Third Baruch (2nd century A.D.)
Fourth Ezra (A.D. 120)

PSALMS

The Psalms of Solomon (50 B.C.)

ETHICS AND WISDOM LITERATURE

Fourth Maccabees (63 B.C.-A.D. 38)
Pirke Aboth (Sayings of the Fathers)
(3rd century B.C.-3rd century A.D.)
Story of Ahikar (500 B.C.)

HISTORY

Fragments of a Zadokite Work (18-8 B.C.)

Dr. R. H. Pfeiffer of Harvard, in his 1953 Introductions to The Apocrypha, agrees in general with Dr. Charles, but makes a few changes in the light of the forty years' scholarship between, dating most of the pseudepigraphic books earlier. Besides, he adds to Dr. Charles' list of the pseudepigrapha the following:

Third Maccabees (about 50 B.C.)
Testament of Job (about 80 B.C.)
Lives of the Prophets (1st century A.D.)
Apocalypse of Abraham (about A.D. 90)

Although Dr. Pfeiffer's book was published late in 1953, there is no mention of the Qumran cave discoveries, probably because he preferred to wait for later evaluation of the manuscripts. So we may infer that his dates above were not influenced by the finds. It will be interesting to see if the "Christian additions" that he finds in six of the pseudepigraphic books are in any originals of them that

55

may be found in the mass of Essene manuscript fragments yet to be identified and translated.

Strangely, Dr. Pfeiffer does not include in his list of the pseudepigraphical books the "Fragments of a Zadokite Work," as Dr. Charles does, although Pfeiffer mentions it in his *Introduction to the Old Testament*, published in 1941.

The Zadokite fragments are often called The Document of Damascus because in the text that city is named as the destination to which the Sons of Zadok fled for refuge from a persecuting ruler (variously identified by scholars), but Damascus may be only a secret name for the Qumran community itself.

The two fragments that Dr. Charles included at the end of his large 1913 collection of pseudepigrapha had been discovered in 1897 in a Cairo Jewish *genizah* (cemetery for worn-out sacred books), but were not translated and published until 1910 by Dr. Schechter of the Jewish Theological Seminary of New York.

No sooner had the *pesher* (interpretation) of Habakkuk from the first cave been examined than it was recognized as closely related to the Zadokite fragments, for it not only reflected a similar point of view and frame of reference, but it also gave the same deferential reverence to the Teacher of Righteousness. So most scholars were not surprised to learn, when some of Qumran Cave 4's great hoard of manuscripts were deciphered, that parts of at least seven different copies of the Zadokite work itself were identified.

Dr. Charles had at first thought of the Cairo manuscripts as being copies of an original work dated between 106 and 57 B.C., but later decided on 18 to 8 B.C. on the basis that the "man of lies" therein referred to was probably Herod the Great, who was King of Judea from 37 to 4 B.C. But the now-recognized close connection of the Zadokite work with the cave Scrolls makes Dr. Charles' original estimate of the earlier date preferable, although the scholars are not all agreed as yet. Dr. Dupont-Sommer, undoubtedly one of the most brilliant scholars working on the problem, places the writing of the Zadokite Document and the Habakkuk Commentary both in the 5th decade B.C. I. Rabinowitz dates it between 175 and 152 B.C. H. H. Rowley says "not later than 131 B.C." and places the other non-Biblical texts (the Habakkuk Commentary, Manual of Discipline, etc.) earlier in the same second century B.C.

7. How Scholars "Protect" Our Faith

Evidently, Millar Burrows belongs to the old school where the measure of a man's scholarship is his reluctance to be definite. He hazards no definite guesses on the date of any manuscript, save that he thinks the Habakkuk Commentary is "one of the younger members of the family of the Dead Sea Scrolls," and "was in all probability written, at the earliest, not very long before 63 B.C., and at the latest not long after that date." (*The Dead Sea Scrolls*, page 186.) And on page 223 he admits that "it now seems to be fairly well established that the non-biblical writings in the scrolls . . . were all composed within a period of about 135 years." (175 B.C-40 B.C.)

What particularly irks anyone who has studied the literature of this whole period, say 175 B.C. to A.D. 50, and its influence on Jesus and his disciples and the beginnings of Christianity is the blithe, nonchalant, and irresponsible way in which the more orthodox Christian scholars (the ones who assure us that the cave findings will not change Christian doctrine one jot or tittle) are restricting the title "The Dead Sea Scrolls" to the larger manuscripts originally found in the first cave by the Bedouin boys. But the "Ark-savers" will admit, if no layman is in hearing, that the "big finds" were in Cave 4, and that "the half has never yet been told."

The real point of the whole discovery is, of course, that the Enochan and other apocalyptic and pseudepigraphic books were found in great profusion in the Qumran caves and can now be dated definitely before Christianity. Their alleged interpolations by Christians can hardly have been made in 100 B.C.

Moreover, the finding of several manuscripts each of Enoch, Jubilees, and the Zadokite Document, the Testament of Levi, and several hitherto unknown pseudepigraphs will be apt to draw the attention of the general Christian public to these noncanonical books. For they are just as new and strange to the great majority of Christians as the more publicized scrolls—the Manual of Discipline, the Thanksgiving Psalms, and the Warfare Book. And, once the more intelligent laity realize the nature of the contents of these pseudepigraphical books, they will be asking embarrassing questions of their pastors and spiritual leaders.

There may be nothing to disturb the faith of the ordinary unobservant Christian who reads the Manual and the Psalms after being assured there is no danger there. Nor is there anything in all the hundreds of cave manuscripts, Enoch and all the rest, to disturb the faith of a Unitarian, for instance, who does not believe in the deity of Jesus, nor in special miraculous revelations, virgin birth, bodily resurrection, salvation, atonement, and similar orthodox dogmas.

And, since most scholars, Christian or Jewish or neither, have either rationalized, or explained casuistically, or completely abandoned belief in miracles and the supernatural, the professed Christians among these scholars can easily say that there is nothing in the Scrolls to disturb their own faith, when, from the point of view of the average lay Christian, these scholars have long since had no faith left to be disturbed!

Right on that very point, too, there needs to be recognized a common error and fallacy. Most people, and this includes not only the average Christian adult but also newspaper and magazine writers and editors, mistakenly suppose that any professor on the faculty of a theological seminary, or a professor teaching "Bible" (Biblical Literature) or Comparative Religion in a college or even in a preparatory school, is a "theologian." And so, since they are theologians, they must necessarily teach theology and, of course, believe what they teach, presumably the Christian faith "once delivered to the saints."

It seems like a little semantic joke to state that today very few theologians teach theology, or even believe in it, save in an extremely theoretical or official way.

Let us digress, though pertinently. On the faculty of any Protestant theological seminary, I care not how orthodox it is supposed to be, you will find at least ten and often twenty professors and teachers of something else for every one professor or assistant professor of theology proper. The chances are that even he will be often called "Professor of the Philosophy of Religion," and will spend more lecture time on philosophy, comparative religion, and the psychology of religion than on the dogmatic theology that is concerned with the doctrines of Christian theology proper—the doctrines that once, and not so long ago, occupied the major part of the curriculum.

The rest of the faculty, euphemistically called "theologians," are professors of Greek and New Testament, professors of Hebrew and Old Testament, professors of Church History, Social Ethics, Missions, Psychology, Comparative Religion, the History of Religion, Religious Education, Clinical Training, Homiletics, Church Music, Sacred Rhetoric, Pastoral Counseling, Liturgics, Patristics, Library Research, Church Administration, and Pastoral Theology. And do not get the idea that the last-named professor teaches any theological doctrines.

Pastoral Theology formerly meant preparing young preachers for visiting homes and teaching the parishioners and their children the doctrines of the church, "instructing the flock in the faith." Now it means many things, none of them doctrinal. It includes teaching the "theologues" how to keep a card index of parishioners' names and addresses, how to prepare a sermon, preach it, then mimeograph it and mail it to the absentees, or tape-record it and run it off in homes of shut-ins or to captive audiences in hospitals and prisons. It even includes training in speech, oral Bible reading, weddings, funerals, church organization, denominational office-holding, group therapy, and publicity and public relations!

All these subjects are necessary nowadays, but why call them "theology," and why call those who teach them "theologians," when most of the faculty members could not pass a simple examination in the doctrines of the church which supports the seminary?

So, when a scholarly professor of Oriental Languages, Comparative Religion, Old Testament, or of Semitic Philology assures you that there is nothing in the Dead Sea Scrolls to disturb Christian faith or change any Christian theological doctrine, just bear in mind that the professor to whom you are listening or whose book you are reading is very likely not a real theologian but a scientifically trained specialist who, if he knows what the doctrines of Christianity are, doesn't really believe in them, unless he is permitted to reinterpret, define, and explain them in his own way.

"Reinterpretation" is a very popular word with the current crop of Christian scholars and professors, and is as useful today as was "that blessed word Mesopotamia" with which early twentieth century preachers covered their timid introduction into their sermons on the Old Testament of the discovery by scholars that Israel's laws and ethics were strangely like those in Babylonian Mesopotamia centuries before Moses. Inasmuch as Abraham had sent his servant into Mesopotamia to get a wife for Isaac, and the result was the beautiful and virtuous Rebekah, and since "dwellers in Mesopotamia" were in the crowd at Pentecost who were baptized "in the name of Jesus Christ," that seemed to make Mesopotamia a blessed link symbolically between the Old Testament and the New, and diverted attention from Hammurabi's presumption in having dared to anticipate the Ten Com-mandments as shown on the great stone stele discovered at Susa in 1902, inscribed with the Code of Hammurabi and even picturing in beautifully wrought diorite bas-relief the king receiving the laws from the hands of his god just as Moses is said to have done almost four centuries later.

Another device used by Christian scholars sometimes when they are forced by scientific discoveries to admit the existence of certain facts apparently dangerous to Christian doctrines as commonly held is to broaden the doctrine of revelation beyond all recognition. Dr. Frank M. Cross, Jr., did this in verbally chastizing Edmund Wilson, whose book on the Dead Sea Scrolls was a best seller, for presuming to think of revelation as a miraculous "suspension of the normal historical process," when anyone "acquainted with contemporary theology" knows that the Christian doctrine of revelation means simply "that God chooses to give meaning to history, not to suspend it." To this most important point we shall refer when further examining the peculiar conduct of the scholars who want to eat their cake and have it too, or, perhaps, who remove the frosting and solemnly assert that the cake was always just plain bread anyway.

8. Bedouins and Harried Savants

To return to the Essene community at Qumran for another, closer look, we find that the report of the contents of Cave 4 throws a great deal more light on these fascinating people.

The discovery of the fourth cave of the Qumran region was, like the first find, due to the Bedouins. With picturesque imagery Dr. Geza Vermes, the brilliant Catholic scholar, whose *Les Manuscrits du Desert de Juda*, published in 1953, was one of the earliest and best of the books on the Qumran manuscripts, tells how the Bedouins would lie low while the scholarly explorers from the French Catholic and American Protestant Schools of Research and Archeology and from the Jewish Palestine Museum would sally forth into the Judean wilderness, loaded with equipment, looking more like an Alpine mountain-climbing expedition than exploring scientists on a field trip. Then the great savants would gingerly climb up and down the patented rope ladders draped over the rocky ledges and crevices, vainly poking into likely-looking fissures and crannies, to the great amusement of invisible sharp-eyed natives.

When the weary searching scientists would finally start back for Jerusalem and home, the ferret-like Bedouins, needing no rope ladders or other fancy equipment, would resume their own tireless probing explorations of all the niches, crevices, and little holes that the scientists had overlooked. For the Bedouins know their own happy hunting grounds and how to get up to and into and down from any part of the rugged terrain; the places called inaccessible by Europeans and Americans merely take a little longer. So, before long, they had "deniched" (to use Vermes' expressive French word) or pried out of the little hole where it had nested for nineteen centuries what was left of a priceless copy of the Zadokite (Damascus) Document.

Let Vermes tell us (in my attempt at rendering his vivid French into English) what happened next:

"But the richest and least expected loot awaited them (the fatigueless ferrets) close by the Qumran ruins. In the grayish marly embankment which, on the east, supports the plateau, a tiny pocketlike hole allured them. At this spot where, normally, nothing should have been preserved, they hit the jackpot—manuscript fragments, large and small, so numerous as to be counted by thousands. . . ."

Once again, therefore, an archeological expedition betook itself in haste to Qumran. The hurried and harried savants were of course elated at another discovery, but rather exasperated that the Bedouins had beaten them to the quarry again.

This time the scientists had the help of the Jordan government's Department of Antiquities in halting the Bedouin diggers, whose activities were dangerous to the fragile manuscript relics. In the last week of September 1952, the scholarly excavators gathered up the comparatively few crumbs the Bedouins had left in this richest of all the caves (known as Cave 4) and also found, close by, Cave 5, intact and containing other manuscript fragments, but these were badly damaged because so thickly encrusted with marl.

The Bedouins could not let the savants take the lead away from them that way, so they promptly found Cave 6, containing better preserved manuscript fragments of leather and even hundreds of fragile papyrus pieces. Fortunately, these were obtained by the scholars before they had passed through too many hands.

Antique dealers in the Behtlehem black market area were apparently quick to catch on to the possibilities of the situation after their fumbling of the Bedouin offering of first finds. At least one of them, according to Father Vermes, has made himself a fortune, buying fragments from the nomad herdsmen and selling them to the scholars at the Palestine Museum.

From the fact that some fragments showed freshly made fractures and tears, it soon dawned on the Wise Men who had come from the West on swift air-camels to Jerusalem that either the Bedouins or the middlemen were making little ones out of big ones, to increase their profits. Rumor had it that the wily sons of the wilderness were even hoarding many of the leather scraps for a rainy day, or until prices should rise still higher. For a time the black market price for fragments was as high as *seven dollars per square inch.*

When the word got around that the purchasers really preferred the larger pieces and would pay more for them, another practice developed. Father Vermes says he saw a lot of fragments arrive at the Palestine Museum about the first of November 1952, some of which had been clumsily pasted together to make bigger pieces.

The scholars have been in a quandary as to how to handle the Bedouins. They have great difficulty dealing with the unscrupulous sons of Ishmael, but cannot very well get along without them either, especially in prospecting for caches of manuscripts and fragments in almost inaccessible places. Yet, unless there is constant supervision, they will conceal their treasure trove, or part of it, from the savants and sell it later on the Bethlehem black market. By the time the crumbling bits of old leather and papyrus finally reach the scholars, not only is the price much higher, but their condition is likely to have deteriorated seriously.

Even if the archeologists offered as much as the black marketeers, it is doubtful if the Bedouins would deal directly with them. In the first place, they have learned that they profit more when they deal through an agent or sell to one of the "antiquarians" of Bethlehem, who will make the foreigners pay a higher price. And besides, these shrewd desert gamins are looking for what fun they can get out of it all too. Unhindered by such peculiar notions as morality, ethics, or loyalty to an employer, they apparently consider it innocent fun to fail to report part of a find, or even all of it, although they may have been employed for that very purpose.

Practically all of the Essene scrolls have been found "less than a stone's throw" from the Qumran Community House, as Dr. Albright has reminded us in reporting this tantalizing news from the archeological front.

Dr. William F. Albright, as the whole scholarly world knows and the rest of the educated world should and soon will know, is the greatest orientalist in this country, if not in the world. He was the scholar to whom Dr. Trever sent the first prints of the first Dead Sea Scroll, Isaiah, and who promptly identified and dated it, congratulating the discoverers. This was March 15, 1948, some time after the Bedouins had found the clay jars in the first Qumran cave.

On May 23rd, 1956, the eve of his sixty-fifth birthday, Dr. Albright gave a memorable address on the Scrolls in the auditorium of the Enoch Pratt Library, the cultural center of Baltimore. As Dr. Albright was the Spence Professor of Semitic Languages at Johns Hopkins University and well beloved in Baltimore, the hall was filled to capacity. He did not indulge in the equivocation and punch-pulling so popular of late among orthodox scholars. He frankly told his fellow townsmen of the very close connection in practices, ideas, and even in the turns of a phrase between the people of the Scrolls, the Essenes, and the early Christians, and that the background of the New

Testament "is far more Jewish than anyone had ever guessed in print, let alone proved." He revealed much more, expressing his opinions as based on his studies, opinions and conclusions of which we shall speak later.

The information he imparted about the difficulties with the Bedouins, which is more apropos of our present subject, is in the report he gave, previously unannounced in this country, that at least two more sheepskin scrolls had been found in the spring of 1956.

The new scrolls were unearthed in the same rocky limestone region, very close to the Qumran settlement, where most of the others were discovered. Guards had been stationed there, but under their very noses the clever Bedouins succeeded in finding and removing these new scrolls and were then holding them until the huge sum they demanded was handed over. How many more scrolls were in their possession was anyone's guess, as they seldom show more than a part of their findings before beginning to deal. Nor does anyone know how many other manuscripts and fragments they have been holding over from previous cave plunderings during the last ten years. The Story of the Dead Sea Scrolls is a serial and will break into the news again and again probably for years.

After the money had been raised to purchase the two or more new scrolls, it would be some time before the public was informed of the general nature of their contents, and still longer till the texts are published (photographed in their original form), then translated and published in modern languages, last of all in English, most likely.

It should be noted that the American public is still waiting for information and translations of manuscripts found in the various caves several years ago, although it is strongly suspected that the scholars immediately concerned have known a great deal about their contents for quite a while.

Of course, the identification of fragments, then collating, photographing, grouping, and translating, and all the other steps of the process take much time, because of the care that must be exercised with the often delicate, minute, and only partly legible pieces. But, allowing for all that, there is still an unnecessarily long time before the public is informed, which can only be accounted for by presuming that the scholars are overly deliberate for one reason or another.

The delay may be due to the rather supercilious professionalism of which ivory-tower people have not been guiltless in the past, or to the similar mental quirk which impels experts, specialists, and "authorities" to withhold new knowledge from the people with the rationalizing excuse that the ignorant populace might use the information to their own harm; or, as has been suspected, the tardiness may be owing to the fact that the new discoveries upset some of the established doctrines of the church, and the savants naturally hesitate to disturb the faith of millions of Christians.

It is entirely possible that the delays which have occurred and are still going on are to be explained by "time out" being taken until advice is secured from ecclesiastical headquarters of some of the several faiths involved. Not that any attempt would be made by the scholars to suppress or destroy any of the documents discovered—a pious practice of former days—but it might be deemed wise, or practical, or "realistic" (to borrow a current political semanticism used to excuse subterfuge), if the scholars consulted with various religious leaders or even among themselves as to just how or when or how much or in what order the contents of the caves should be revealed.

Certainly there must already have been considerable

hesitation before some passages in the Scrolls now accessible in English translations were exposed to the startled gaze of the righteous saints and the smiles of the sinners and infidels.

Dr. Albright is of the opinion (so he said in Baltimore) that the Scrolls were slow to come to public attention because they interfered with certain pet theories of various scholars rather than because of dogmatic theology.

Postponing comment for ten years or even fifty until more of the fragments had been inspected, classified, and translated was a popular attitude at first among the New Testament scholars, who were asked to predict the effect of the Scrolls on Christian doctrines and the faith of the layman. They were following Josh Billings' advice: "Don't never prophesy onless ye know."

But that bluff has been called. Said Dr. A. Powell Davies, the late famed preacher of All Souls' Church, Unitarian, of Washington, D.C., speaking apropos of the "too-early-yet-to-draw-any inferences; wait-fifty-years" school of New Testament professors:

"This is indeed an amiable suggestion. In fifty years our present New Testament scholars will no longer be teaching and can hand on the problems of the Dead Sea Scrolls to their unfortunate successors." And Dr. Davies asserts trenchantly that the professors themselves well knew but were avoiding the fact that there is enough known already of and about the Essene literature found in the caves for the formation of a preliminary interpretation and a temporary opinion which can be changed later if new facts warrant it.

I might add from my own continuous contacts with New Testament professors, which began in 1905, that all through these fifty years I have never found these learned gentlemen either slow or reluctant to offer hypothetical interpretations and opinionative theories—and moreover based on far less documentary material than the Dead Sea Scrolls offered about 10 years ago, when the reverend fathers were playing so coy and shy about saying anything regarding the manuscripts except perhaps that there was nothing to fear, for "the grass withereth, the flower fadeth, but the word of our God shall stand forever."

9. Why Was America Kept in the Dark So Long?

Were these defenders of the faith "speaking comfortably to Jerusalem" (as advised in the 2nd verse of the 40th chapter of Isaiah) by quoting the 8th verse which predicts that the word of God shall stand forever? If their hearers and readers understood by that "comfort" (as all orthodox Christians do), that nothing, not even the Dead Sea Scrolls, would change the infallible revealed Word of God, the Bible, then it was quite a coincidence that fifteen corrections had already been made in that very book of Isaiah by the insertion of readings from the Dead Sea manuscript of Isaiah in the place of discarded passages in the King James Version!

Dr. Millar Burrows had listed the variant readings in the "St. Mark's" Isaiah manuscript from the first Qumran cave on his way back from Palestine, and turned his notes over to the Old Testament section of the Revised Standard Bible Committee that met at Northfield, Massachusetts, in the summer of 1948. The "R.S.V." was published four years later in September 1952, but nothing was told the public about the fifteen Dead Sea Scrolls' insertions in Isaiah until 1955, three years after publication, and, be it noted, after the appearance of Edmund Wilson's revealing piece in The New Yorker.

When that "news" roused the laymen, who in turn roused their preachers to a recognition of the unexplained delay in getting information about the interpretation of the Scrolls to the American public, Dr. Theodore A. Gill, editor of The Christian Century, vigorously condemned "the unforgivable scholarly reticence which had kept us in the dark too long."

But the editors of the various American denominational and undenominational Christian weeklies should not have put so much of the burden of blame on the Old and New Testament scholars and professors. They should have gallantly shared that shame of long delay.

Is it possible that there are no persons on the staffs of our denominational journals assigned to keep posted on European publications containing important news of the Christian world? Can no American editors read French? Or German? Or Swedish?

For Dupont-Sommer's Paris publishers, Adrien-Maisonneuve, had brought out his *Preliminary Studies of the Dead Sea Manuscripts* in 1950, and his *Remarks on the Habakkuk Commentary* the same year, his *Remarks on the Manual of Discipline* in 1951, and his fairly complete and very stimulating *New Studies of the Dead Sea Manuscripts* in 1953; all these in French, of course. Delcor had two books on the Scrolls published in Paris in 1951. Vermes had one published in 1951, and his very fine *The Manuscripts of the Judean Desert* with ample introduction, comments, translations, and bibliography in 1953. Reicke's Swedish book *Manuscripts from Qumran* was out in 1952. In German we had Kahle's very interesting *The Hebrew Manuscripts from the Caves* in 1951, and the next year Hans Bardtke's popular *The Manuscript Find by the Dead Sea*, was a second edition brought up to date in 1953.

Besides these widely circulated "regular" books, there were literally hundreds of articles in journals and quarterlies in the French, Swedish, Spanish and Italian beginning in 1948 and 1949, and some of them making statements more startling than any uttered by Wilson or Dupont-Sommer.

But even if American preachers and editors of church papers were illiterate save in the English tongue, there were several articles and even books available in that language long before the editor of *The New Yorker* got his bright idea to give Edmund Wilson his assignment.

But books in English about the Qumran manuscripts —what few there were—could not be found in American bookshops. The American Schools of Oriental Research in New Haven published in 1950 volume one, and in 1951, part 2 of volume two, of *The Dead Sea Scrolls of St. Mark's Monastery* (Qumran), but while these had English titles, they were simply plates of photographic reproductions of the Isaiah manuscript, the Habakkuk Commentary, and the Manual of Discipline, all in Hebrew, of course, with a brief introduction in English in volume one.

In 1951, Oxford University Press published in London under the title, *The Hebrew Scrolls from the Neighborhood of Jericho and the Dead Sea*, a thin volume containing a lecture of the previous year by G. R. Driver, advocating a late date (A.D. 200-500) for the Scrolls, a theory since disproved. In 1952, Blackwell at Oxford published an English translation of Dupont-Sommer's first book, calling it simply *The Dead Sea Scrolls*, and in 1954 in London, Vallentine, Mitchell & Co. brought out in English his second book, entitling it *The Jewish Sect of Qumran and the Essenes*.

H. H. Rowley's excellent *The Zadokite Fragments and the Dead Sea Scrolls* was published by Blackwell at Oxford in 1952, and in the same year in New York by The Macmillan Company. Unfortunately, the book was two-thirds notes, references, and bibliography. And in its brief concentrated text it presumed such an acquaintance with already published European books and Journal articles on the Scrolls, and was written in such technical theological jargon well sprinkled with Hebrew, Greek, Latin, French, and German words and quotations, that it might as well have been set up in Mayan hieroglyphics or demotic Egyptian as far as American readers were concerned.

When, however, The Macmillan Company got the American rights and published in New York the fine English translation by Dr. Rowley's daughter of the first Dupont-Sommer book, *The Dead Sea Scrolls*, which was illustrated, well written, and contained beautiful English renderings of Dupont-Sommer's vivid French translations of some of the actual cave manuscripts, then a few people here, apparently including the editor of *The New Yorker*, began to sit up and take notice.

It is one of the most surprising of the many unexpected incidents connected with the discovery, appraisal, and publication of the Scrolls that the first information concerning the epochal find reached the American public from a literary man, Edmund Wilson, rather than from a Biblical scholar, archeologist, or theologian.

Be all that as it may, it was *The New Yorker* article, "The Scrolls from the Dead Sea," appearing in the issue of May 15, 1955, over eight years after the first Scroll discovery, that awakened Americans to the startling fact that something had happened in Palestine of vastly more importance than the perpetual tribal quarrels over boundaries. The general public of America, including nearly all the best educated and most cultured classes, had never even heard of *The Biblical Archaelogist* or the *Bulletin of the American Schools of Oriental Research*, which had carried in late 1948 and during 1949 the first American scholarly reports of the Scroll finds.

Dr. Millar Burrows states on page 18 of his book *The Dead Sea Scrolls* that "interested scholars were . . . fairly well informed on the general nature and contents of the Scrolls within a year" after he first learned of their existence (which was a year after they were found), but that statement needs considerable qualification. Only a few scholars, very few in America, knew much of anything about any of the Scrolls then (March 1949), and the big find in Cave 4, recognized by scholars as the most important, was not made, much less translated, until three and a half years later, September 1952.

Note that Dr. Burrows' book was not published until 1955, three years after that, and yet he did not correct that statement on page 18, evidently because he and several others of the orthodox "Ark-protectors" persist in confining and limiting the term "Dead Sea Scrolls" to the inscribed rolls found in the first cave. That makes it easier to say that there is nothing in the Scrolls to disturb anyone's faith. It is part of the hush-hush policy.

When Edmund Wilson came in contact with Dr. Dupont-Sommer, he found a great scholar who not only knew the significance of the finds but would talk to an adroit reporter, and he furnished much of the theological dynamite that exploded in The New Yorker piece. Consequently there was a sudden demand for the books of the savant Wilson implied was a reincarnation of Ernst Renan (the brilliant heretic of nearly a century ago); and Dupont-Sommer's first book was sold out immediately, while his second, The Jewish Sect of Qumran and the Essenes, published here August 30, 1955, slightly corrected the first and expanded it, by adding more dynamite. It is a brilliant constructive work of fine scholarship.

Professor A. Dupont-Sommer of the Sorbonne, specialist there in Hebrew, is also director of studies at the Ecole des Hautes Etudes at the University of Paris. He perceives almost at once the significance of any new discovery in all its aspects (as does our equally eminent American scholar Dr. Albright), but he is also very clever and subtle in argument and controversy, so that his opponents sometimes think he is giving in to them when he is only adding to their eventual discomfiture, as will be indicated when we get to the chapter on how the Scrolls affect the Bible and Christian doctrine. His critics are apt to lay to sheer luck the disconcerting frequency with which his rather heretical theories turn out to be correct, although

75

he seemed to be basing those theories on passages that did not warrant his inferences and deductions.

Dupont-Sommer was quick to perceive that the Qumran sect of the New Covenant must be recognized as Essenes, and said so in his first book (1950), while other scholars quibbled on that point till long after. Naturally, following Renan's theory that the apocryphal and pseudepigraphical Jewish literature between the Testaments included ideas commonly supposed to be original with Christianity, Dupont-Sommer went further. He said that not only the Book of Jubilees and the Books of Enoch but also "many other writings figuring amongst the 'Pseudepigrapha of the Old Testament' should likewise be assigned to the sect of the New Covenant, in particular the 'Testaments of the Twelve Patriarchs,' to which the 'Damascus (Zadokite) Document' alludes many times, the 'Assumption of Moses,' the 'Psalms of Solomon,' and indeed certain of the Apocrypha."

When Dupont-Sommer wrote his second book, he returned to this very important matter (neglected by other scholars) of the connection of the Qumran Essenes and the Pseudepigrapha, recalling that in 1950 "a Hebrew fragment of 'Jubilees' had already been recognized among the manuscripts found in 1947. Since then," he continued (page 38), "a Hebrew fragment of 'Enoch' has been identified; hence 'Jubilees' and 'Enoch' formed part of the library of the Dead Sea monastery of the Essenes."

He was not too sure that this latter Hebrew fragment was really from Enoch, for in a footnote he added: "At least the identification is very probable." But, as usual, his hunch about Enoch was abundantly justified a little later; also his slim basis on Jubilees, when large fragments of several manuscripts of both books were identified from Cave 4, giving a firm foundation to his pregnant appraisal of the real historical significance of the finds in the Qumran caves:

"The importance of the discoveries beside the Dead Sea

from the historical aspect is not only that they have given us previously unknown Essene writings, but also that they have allowed us to obtain, thanks to these writings, a more exact and certain understanding of these 'Pseudepigrapha' which completed the Bible of the Essenes, and which were uncertain in their interpretation at many points by reason of their esoteric character."

It is right here, where Dupont-Sommer says that the Pseudepigrapha (Jubilees, Enoch, Testaments of the Twelve Patriarchs, etc.) "completed the Bible of the Essenes," that we have the recognition by a great scholar of perhaps the most important fact revealed by the discoveries in the Qumran caves. This is the fact that Enoch and the other pseudepigraphic and apocalyptic Jewish literature is of Essene origin, part of the Bible of the Qumran Essene community, and is found in scroll form in the Dead Sea caves, written in the same language by the same people at the same time as the Manual of Discipline, the Zadokite Document, or any other of the more publicized scrolls of the Qumran caves.

Now, note carefully what Dr. Millar Burrows does in his book *The Dead Sea Scrolls*. On page 330, he argues against Dupont-Sommer's idea that Jesus seemed "in many respects an astonishing reincarnation of the Teacher of Righteousness," pictured in the Habakkuk Commentary scroll. Dr. Burrows unfairly omitted the qualifying phrase "in many respects," in Dr. Dupont-Sommer's original statement, but was not as tricky as Father Petrus Nober and the French scholar, M. Delcor, both of whom have Dupont-Sommer saying Jesus was "nothing but an astonishing reincarnation." Dupont-Sommer naturally protested (page 161) the "nothing but" insertion when he wrote his second book, *The Jewish Sect of Qumran and the Essenes*, which appeared in French in 1953 and in English in 1954, over a year before Burrows' book.

But the prize sentence in Dr. Burrows' book is on page 331. After discounting all Dupont-Sommer's parallels between Jesus and the Teacher of Righteousness, and the alleged similarities in their ethical teachings, Dr. Burrows says that the differences between the Dead Sea Scrolls and the sayings of Jesus concerning the future are "even more striking." Then, in the same paragraph, he says: "In general the sayings of Jesus are related to the apocalyptic literature of Judaism more closely than to anything in the scrolls."

To such a balmily benign assertion, one can only reply:

"But, dear Dr. Burrows, regarding this 'apocalyptic literature of Judaism' (which you admit is closely related to the sayings of Jesus, more so 'than to anything in the scrolls')—you know very well that it includes and is mainly represented by the Enochan and the related apocalypses. Where did it come from? Was it not also of Essene origin? Was it not written by, copied by, published by, read by, studied by, and preserved in these very caves by these Essenes of the great cultural and literary center which we have, at long last, discovered?

"The Essene authorship of the Enochan literature was maintained by many eminent scholars long before the Qumran manuscripts were discovered and is now confirmed by the neat way in which the sectarian scrolls such as the Rule of the Community and the Habakkuk Commentary dovetail into, complement, and explain the ideas, doctrines, and the very language of the Enochan books, Jubilees and the Testaments of the Twelve Patriarchs, which also return the compliment.

"And so, Dr. Burrows, when you rewrite and update your book, The Dead Sea Scrolls, please remember that The Books of Enoch and Jubilees and the Testaments are just as much entitled to be called the Dead Sea Scrolls as the Rule of the Community, which you baptized The Manual of Discipline."

A rather amusing development has taken place that further justifies the right of The Books of Enoch and "Jubilees" to be included among the Scrolls, even if that sacred literary aristocracy be limited to those found in Cave 1 in 1954 by the first shepherds. In that cave they found and later sold eleven scrolls or large fragments, representing when reunited seven different manuscripts. Dr. Burrows, on page 19 of his book, inaccurately reckons them as six, counting the two variant Isaiah manuscripts as one.

But Fate dealt him a joker among the sacred six cards. Number 4 in his list of the Scrolls is given as tentatively named the "Lamech Scroll, which has not yet been unrolled." Well, now it has been, and parts of its contents have been officially published in a beautiful volume. It took a long time. One reason given for the delay of almost a decade is that the roll was all gummed up and stuck together. Parts of it were very sticky—in more ways than one—and both ways probably contributed to the delay in publication, judging from the scholarly scuttlebutt in circulation three years ago when le monde savant already had a pretty good idea of the contents.

The "joker" among the sacred six scrolls of Cave 1 is this very "Lamech Scroll" or "Book of Lamech," now rebaptized "A Genesis Apocryphon" by its editors and translators, Nahman Avigad and Yigael Yadin. At this writing, we do not yet have the text or translation of the entire scroll, for the mutilated condition of many of its twenty-two columns requires many months yet of patient work, but "this preliminary survey," as the editors term it, does give us columns 20, 21, and 22 practically complete, with most of columns 19 and 2, plus hints and clever guesses as to the probable contents of the other columns. And what is already known definitely places this scroll as typical Enochan pseudepigraphical literature.

Repeatedly the editors comment on the resemblance of verses and sections of the Apocryphon text verbatim to or slightly variant from The Book of Enoch and The Book of Jubilees. Fifteen times they mention the former and sixty-eight times the latter, which will certainly give Du-

79

pont-Sommer another chance to smile at the vindication of one more of his precocious guesses. Contrary to several other scholars, he held to the Essene origin of the books of "Enoch" and "Jubilees." And as long ago as 1950, he had predicted that this very scroll from Cave 1, which was then still tightly rolled (and being vainly offered for sale in the United States) and was tentatively named "The Book of Lamech" or simply the "Lamech Scroll," would be found to be "certainly connected with the writings of Enoch, which would thus themselves be brought into relation with the sect of the New Covenant" at Qumran.

Dupont-Sommer at that time (1950) had mere scraps of evidence from the caves to back up his theory of the Qumran origin of the two books. But the finding of eight partial manuscripts of Enoch and five of Jubilees in Cave 4 in 1952, plus fragments of both when the debris of Cave 1 was finally sifted (together with the announcement of the real character of the sixth scroll from Cave 1 as full of Enochan and other similar pseudepigraphic writings), increase Dupont-Sommers' reputation as a really fine scholar who is more often right than are his critics.

In order to understand the real meaning and revolutionary significance of the discovery of the Dead Sea Scrolls, we must repeatedly call attention to the very important fact that the non-Biblical writings, (including mainly apocalyptic, pseudepigraphic, and apocryphal books) thus far found in the many Qumran cave caches, and found long before Dr. Burrows' book was published in 1955, greatly outnumber the seven books in eleven scrolls or parts of scrolls discovered by the Bedouins in the first cave in 1947, to which Dr. Burrows apparently confines the phrase "Dead Sea Scrolls." And even when you take note of the interesting fact that parts of every book in the Jewish Bible, called the Old Testament by the Christians, have been found in the Qumran caves (with the significant exception of the Book of Esther), you must still admit and ponder the more interesting and important fact that in the same caves, and inextricably mixed with the fragments of the canonical books, there have been found twice as many scrolls and fragments of the apocalyptic Enochan literature and its general type of non-canonical books.

Why is not everything of a written nature found in the same cave region entitled to be called part of the Dead Sea Scrolls?

One could account for this peculiarity as a mere oversight were it not for others we have noted and shall mention. Before we get through we may find the reason why the great corpus of the Enochan literature is today being played down, ignored, and shoved to one side, while less important but much "safer" writings are given the spotlight. It is the same old reason why it was gradually pushed out of the collection of sacred books by over-zealous defenders of orthodoxy during the period when the canon of official scripture was being determined.

Unfortunately, that authorized list of approved writings was not determined by historical facts but by theological considerations. During the early Christian centuries, when there grew up the body of doctrine, the process of acceptance by the various churches was steered by the presbyters and bishops toward an increasingly orthodox and conservative corpus of creed in which the supernatural and the miraculous predominated and the human element was subordinated.

A "scheme of salvation" emerged, transforming the man Jesus into the mystical Christ, the Son of God.

This scheme represented Jesus' advent as a miracle, a break in the continuity of history, a sudden thrusting into the material world by God of His only Son, to be born miraculously of a virgin through the magic power of the Holy Spirit. Instead of portraying Jesus as he had really

81

been, a splendid example of the best type of Jewish thinker of his day, he was declared to have been something new and infinitely better than anyone who had ever lived before. Compared with him, even the great prophets of Israel were unimportant, save as their teachings could be twisted to prove that they predicted his coming, and what he would be like. He was to be the "bright and morning star," so the people of Jesus' day were pictured in dark colors as full of sin and all manner of wickedness, as if he suddenly arrived from heaven like a bright comet against the black background of Judaism.

In the body of doctrine as it grew, influenced by current ideas about what a god-man should be and do, Jesus must perforce have come from heaven to be born of a virgin, must perform many miracles, make mystic utterances, raise the dead occasionally, and then himself die, rise again from the dead, and be assumpted back to heaven, thus proving his deity from advent to ascension. These were the standard "signs" by which a new god could be recognized, and these myths were gradually attached to the person of Jesus the son of Miryam (Mary) as his deification proceeded.

Today, in liberal Christian theological circles, little known to the general public, a whole school of professional theologians led by Dr. Rudolf Bultmann has been at work for some time in the attempt to save Christianity by a technical process known in Germany as *Entmythologesierung*, which is usually but not quite accurately translated "demythologizing." It means rather the releasing of Christianity from the burden of maintaining that these typical deification myths are *literally* true, while at the same time preserving their symbolical, esoteric, and psychological values.

Obviously, the early Christian church "Fathers" (teaching bishops and theologians) had their work cut out for them when they set out to "mythologize" Jesus into an acceptable new god by "dehumanizing" him, especially when they had to have him human during his earthly sojourn so that he could really suffer and die as an atonement sacrifice to appease the wrath of God, his heavenly Father! But theology thrives on inconsistencies that have to be explained and reconciled, otherwise the theologians would join the ranks of the unemployed. The earlier ones, however, were kept pretty busy.

For one thing, they had to work hard for a long time at the task of removing as "doubtful, heretical, spurious, and rejected" any writings, however popular and beloved of the layfolk, which might cast doubt on this theological interpretation of the birth, education, beliefs, sayings, teachings, healings, life and death of Jesus the Christ, the newly revealed Son of God and Saviour of the World. Fortunately, they did not do a very thorough job and left enough seams showing, and enough scraps of material around, for our modern scientific scholars to piece things together and give several good guesses as to the real nature and teaching of the human Jesus. Now the scientists, in the light of the Qumran discoveries, can get much closer to that remarkable young man who emerged from "the wilderness" to give to the world his synthesis of the wisdom, faith and hopes of several cultures he had studied in the remarkable community and its wonderful library by the shore of the Salty Sea.

Another, related task faced the early Christianity-makers: there must especially be cast out of the church-approved collection of scriptures any books of the Jews, written before "Christ" came, which contained ethical teachings and doctrinal beliefs too close to his and expressed in words and phrases too often found in his vocabulary. That meant that many of the writings of the second and first centuries B.C. and of the first half of the first century A.D. would have to be discarded. They were, but many of them have turned up at Qumran!

And any references to such writings had to be edited

out of the otherwise approved holy books. Here, too, the eliminators missed a few telltale verses, like Jude 14:, or let their patchwork show, as in First Peter 3:18-20, which we shall prove a little later.

10. Importance of Enoch and Other Pseudepigraphs

The Book of Enoch was obviously inconvenient to have around in the fourth century A.D. when Christian doctrines were being shaped up. Its vocabulary and ethics and theology were all too much like those of Jesus and the Gospel writers who had quoted him. Besides, the Enochan literature had featured and Jesus had adopted, applied to himself, and definitely and repeatedly promised to his disciples the "end of the world" idea with the "second coming" of the Son of Man on the clouds of heaven; but by the third and fourth centuries, this "Kingdom Come" had not come and "this generation" of his immediate disciples had long since passed away. So, any reminder of that unfulfilled promise of Jesus, however casuistically it might be reinterpreted or explained away, was embarrassing to have around.

To excise all the many verses in which Jesus promised to return ere that generation passed away was too drastic editing, but, at any rate, it was just as well to push to one side such unnecessary emphasis on the idea of the return of the Son of Man as was afforded by the Enochan apocalypse. Let the fanatics who liked violent apocalyptic imaginative writing be content with John's Apocalypse, the strange vision he said he had on the Isle of Patmos. One such book in the canon was enough. Why include that troublesome Book of Enoch?"

Enoch is even more disturbing to orthodox theologians right now, for today there are more doctrines to reconcile with it; and "eschatology" (the doctrines of the "last

85

things" to occur at the end of the world) is very much discussed in Fundamentalist Christian circles because of the menace of the atom bomb.

Moreover, it is extremely embarrassing to read the best part of the Sermon on the Mount, for instance, in the Enochan and other similar Essene writings, such as Jubilees, the Psalms of Solomon, and the Testaments of the Twelve Patriarchs, when we have found actual pre-Christian manuscripts of them in Cave 4, right in the backyard of the Essene Qumran house!

Here are these "rejected" books, written B.C., yet containing many sayings and teachings hitherto thought by most Christians to be original in Christianity's New Testament, and to have been first spoken by Jesus the Christ as a direct new revelation, a hitherto-unrevealed message from God the Father!

Consider also, as an important factor in the problem now facing the reluctant Christian world, a fact not featured or even mentioned in the articles written by the apologists who pooh-pooh the importance of the Scrolls findings—namely, that certain of the oldest existing manuscripts of the New Testament, dating from the fourth, fifth, and sixth centuries A.D., included the noncanonical books of the Psalms of Solomon, the Epistle of Barnabas, and the Shepherd of Hermas. All these were later excluded from the official Bible. Why?

Very probably the reason why they are not in our Bible, although considered sacred scripture by the early Church, is that all three had some connection with the Essenes. The Psalms of Solomon were written about 50 B.C., very likely at Qumran, for it has the same attitude toward the Temple and the priests as the Manual of Discipline, and much resembles the psalms found in Cave 1. It is obviously Essenic and it was no surprise to scholars when fragments of it were found at Qumran.

The eighteen beautiful psalms attributed pseudepigraphically to Solomon were widely circulated in Jesus' day and it is possible that he quoted from them. Certainly the cup of strong wine God gave men to drink (Psalm Sol. 8:15) seems to be recalled by Jesus in Gethsemane when he prays, "O my Father, if it be possible, let this cup pass away from me: nevertheless, not as I will, but as thou wilt" (Matthew 26:39), and as they left the garden when he told Peter to put up his sword, and said: ". . . the cup which the Father hath given me, shall I not drink it?" (John 18:11.)

In that same Gethsemane agony, when Jesus said to Peter, James and John: "My soul is exceeding sorrowful, even unto death: abide ye here and watch" (Mark 14:34), he came back presently only to find (verse 40) "them sleeping, for their eyes were very heavy." It may well be that here we have a sort of sorrowful echo of the first two verses of the 16th Psalm of Solomon: ". . . sunk in the heaviness of them that slumber far from God . . . my soul had been wellnigh poured out unto death."

Parallels cannot be forced, but any person familiar with the Gospel writings cannot read the Psalms of Solomon without being frequently reminded of Jesus, his words, ideas, and inspirations. The book belongs in our Bible, but it was apparently excluded by the Christians as too Essenic, and by the Jews as too Christian.

As for the so-called "Epistle of Barnabas," an anonymous work of the late first or early second century A.D., Christendom is poorer because this very inspiring twenty-one-chapter book was excluded from the finally authorized and accepted canon of Scripture. If the earlier date of A.D. 70-77 maintained by good scholarship be accepted for its composition, it is earlier than several canonical books, and the conjectural later date of A.D. 117 still places it among the earliest of the compositions of the Apostolic Fathers.

The "Epistle of Barnabas" was esteemed as canonical in several early churches: Clement of Alexandria quotes it as Scripture, and Origen terms it a "Catholic Epistle." Most significant of all is its appearance in the fourth century *Codex Sinaiticus*, our oldest (with the possible exception of *Vaticanus*) and most complete manuscript of the Bible, both Old and New Testaments. Here it is placed immediately after the book of Revelation, and is definitely included in the New Testament.

We have emphasized the early prestige of Barnabas in order to call attention to the pressure that must have been exerted to have it removed from its place of authority. There can be little doubt that its disappearance was largely, if not wholly, due to its very obvious featuring of Essenic ideas and its open recognition of the Book of Enoch as authoritative Scripture.

In the Epistle of Barnabas 16:5, the author states: "For the Scripture says, 'And it shall come to pass in the last days that the Lord shall deliver the sheep of his pasture, and the sheep-fold, and their tower to destruction.'" This is from the Book of Enoch chapter 89, verses 55, 66, and 67, in condensed form. The Barnabas chapter 16, moreover, in which this quotation from Enoch occurs, is itself concerned with the Temple at Jerusalem and reveals the typical Essenic attitude toward it, which Jesus had himself earlier adopted.

But in chapter four Barnabas comes right out and names Enoch as his authority, prefacing "as Enoch says," to his condensation of parts of chapters 89 and 90 of the Book of Enoch.

The most striking Essenic brand or hallmark in Barnabas, however, is one that was very plain in early Christian days, but that we would hardly have recognized before the Qumran caves gave us "The Warfare of the Sons of Light against the Sons of Darkness." In the 18th, 19th, and 20th chapters of the Epistle of Barnabas is one of the finest codes of conduct in any scripture, a blending of the Ten Commandments and the Sermon on the Mount. And the section is introduced by the typically Essenic formula (found not only in the "Warfare" book, but very clearly in Second Enoch as well): "There are two ways of teaching and power, one of Light and one of Darkness . . . over the one are set light-bringing angels of God, but over the other angels of Satan."

When the churches threw out the beautiful and inspiring Epistle of Barnabas—ostensibly to get rid of its Jewish Essenic contents, character, and atmosphere—they certainly threw out the baby with the bath, or cut off their nose to spite their face. Worse still, they deprived a hundred generations since of a book better than some innocuous, orthodox, un-Essenic books they carefully saved.

Now, in the same ancient *Codex Sinaiticus* which contains the Epistle of Barnabas is part (one-fourth) of another book much beloved of the early Christians, the "Shepherd of Hermas." For this old manuscript (rescued by Tischendorf from the waste pile with which the monks of Mount Sinai fed their fireplaces), the British people in 1933 gave their sixpences and pennies to raise the half-million dollars to buy for the British Museum the *Codex Sinaiticus* from the U.S.S.R., whose government had found it in the Imperial Library of St. Petersburg, where it had been deposited after Tischendorf persuaded the monks of Mt. Sinai to present it to Tsar Nicholas II.

Of course the Shepherd of Hermas, that delightful if somewhat puritanical chap, had to go too, for he was daubed with the same Essenic taint, according to the orthodox guardians of the "faith once delivered to the saints" (but frequently edited by the saints to save the sinners).

His exclusion from the canon may have been due to the opening two verses of the Hermas story where the hero, then a slave, sees his lady owner bathing in the River Tiber and in helping her out of the river notes her great beauty; or the later episode where he spends a day and a night with twelve beautiful maidens, kissing, embracing, and dancing by day and praying all night. But there is much excellent moral instruction in the book, which was really a second century A.D. forerunner of *Pilgrim's Progress*. Also the slightly sexy parts are so much tamer than certain incidents still remaining in the canonical books that it must have been for some other reason it was banned.

And Hermas is now seen, in the light of the Scrolls, to have been much more likely to have been written by an Essene, or an Essenic-educated author, than by the Christian brother of Pius, Bishop of Rome, who, according to tradition and an early church authority, is said to have written it somewhere about A.D. 150. Or this traditional author may have been more of an Essene in his theology than his official bishop-brother suspected.

At any rate, the Essenic character of the book is evident from many indications—its apocalyptic form; its visions, commands, and similitudes so much like the Book of Enoch; its many angels; its emphases on baptism, chastity, temperance, prophecy, the Holy Spirit, the Second Coming, eschatology, and many other doctrines. More noticeable, perhaps, is the fact that the names "Jesus" or "Christ" do not occur anywhere in the book. There are several minor indications leaning toward Essenism, such as a fondness for the symbolism and Gnosticism of John's Gospel, and a remarkable acquaintance with and frequent quotation from the epistles of James and Hebrews.

Because of all these resemblances, Hermas has become one of the books on which the Scrolls discoveries have focused attention. Now that the hypothesis of Essene authorship is being considered seriously, although rather tardily and reluctantly, problems in and about this neglected book that have puzzled scholars for centuries are apparently in the process of solution. It is being recalled that as early as A.D. 177, Irenaeus, Bishop of Lyons, accepted the book as Scripture. Origen, in his *Commentary on Romans* written about A.D. 245, called the book very useful and, he thought, divinely inspired. He attributed its authorship to the Hermas whom Paul mentions as a member of the Roman Church in A.D. 58 (Epistle to the Romans, 16:14), and while that date may be too early, it must now be reconsidered.

So, we see today that these books, The Psalms of Solomon, The Epistle of Barnabas, and the apocalypse The Shepherd of Hermas, although included in our oldest and most complete Bible manuscript, *Codex Sinaiticus*, of the fourth century A.D., were excluded from the slowly evolving Christian Bible (Old and New Testaments). Probably this was because they were witnesses in one way or another to the Jewish Essene influence, especially the Enochan part, on Jesus and the early church. The Books of Enoch themselves were thoroughly eliminated and deemed "lost."

No one yet knows how many books of Enoch there were in circulation in Jesus' day. Until 1855, when Ewald, the great German scholar, detected evidence of several authors, they were all supposed to be only one *The Book of Enoch.* The existence of even that one was known to observant Bible readers for centuries only because of the reference to it by name in the New Testament book of Jude, which we now know had a hard time getting into the canon for that very reason!

St. John the Divine's "Revelation" also had difficulty getting in, because it was apocalyptic; that is, it predicted the future in a peculiar style of writing where strange symbolic animals and angels, good and bad, fought each other. By the end of the fourth century, apocalypses were going out of style anyway, since Jesus hadn't "come quickly," so in the contest for official approval, Revelation just barely overcame its handicap of being so much like Enoch.

Apart from the reference to Enoch in Jude all noticeable traces of that once popular book and its kindred apocalytical and sapiential (wisdom) books were in time removed. A rather thorough job of suppression was done. To be sure, there were many quotations from the excluded books left in, to say nothing of their doctrines, but as long as the names of the books were not given, and since quotation marks had not been invented, how were the people, or the clergy, to know which verses were Enochan quotations if no copies of Enoch were available?

Orthodox theologians would have us believe that "Enoch" sort of lost itself: that is, that no council or group of bishops chose certain books and left out others. Some books were popular and remained in the collection of Scriptures; others were not universally popular and gradually just dropped out of circulation, earlier in some places than in others. Thus, the "canon" or list of accepted Scriptures became official by an almost miraculous process of self-authentication, led and supervised, of course, by the Holy Spirit.

This is a pretty theory and widely accepted today, especially by Christians not familiar with church history, or the secular history by which church histories published by the churches must continually be corrected.

The greatest authority on Enoch was and still is Canon R. H. Charles, who was more of a scholar than a churchman and fought his fellow-clergy many years, insisting on the very great importance of the Book of Enoch and its related apocalyptic writings "as being practically the only historical memorials of the religious development of Judaism from 200 B.C. to 100 A.D., and particularly of the development of that side of Judaism to which historically Christendom in large measure owes its existence."

Those were fighting words in 1913 when they were published in Dr. Charles' huge two-volume *Apocrypha and Pseudepigrapha of the Old Testament*, vol. 2, page 163.

They were singularly prophetic, as is apparent today when they are underlined and italicized by the finding of copies of Enoch and the other pseudepigrapha in the Qumran caves, along with the other Essene books which so well supplement them with additional evidence that "that side of Judaism" was Essenism from which Christianity derived.

The Book of Enoch was very popular for at least 500 years. It was certainly popular among the Essenes of Qumran, for more copies are turning up there regularly. Jesus and his biographers must have loved it. They quoted much from it and adopted its doctrines and beliefs, as we shall see in a later chapter. With Paul it is said to have been his vade mecum, literally his "go with me," his pocketbook, his manual for frequent reference.

Dr. Charles pointed out that "nearly all the writers of the New Testament were familiar with it, and were more or less influenced by it in thought and diction. . . . With the earlier Fathers and Apologists it had all the weight of a canonical book."

Nevertheless, when the theology-obsessed bishops of the fourth century A.D. sharpened their busy orthodox shears at the First Council of Nicaea, A.D. 325, and proclaimed that being a Christian meant belief that Jesus was deity just as much as God the Father was, it was only a matter of time before Enoch would be entirely shorn from Holy Scripture. Against the doctrine of a supernatural revelation of new truth in Christ (a doctrine inseparable from the deity of Jesus), the Book of Enoch was too revealing of what was for all practical purposes a very good sort of pre-Christian Christianity. That would never do!

So, as Dr. Charles points out, after having been recognized as Scripture by Jude in the first century A.D., Enoch had ample recognition in the second century by Barnabas and Athenagoras, and in the third century by Clement of Alexandria, by Irenaeus, and Tertullian; but "from the fourth century of our era onward it fell into discredit, and under the ban of Hilary, Jerome, and Augustine it gradually passed out of circulation and became lost to the knowledge of Western Christendom. . . ." (Charles' *The Book of Enoch or 1 Enoch*, 1912, page six.)

But men of many nations and all walks of life liked Enoch because it had answers for the questions that were being asked all over the then-known world—questions that had risen in the minds of men awakened by the wide-ranging fertilizing influence of Hellenism, the conquering culture of Alexander the Great. As Dr. Charles says (page x) in his great book:

"The Book of Enoch . . . comes from many writers and almost as many periods. It touches upon every subject that could have arisen in the ancient schools of the prophets, but naturally it deals with these subjects in an advanced stage of development. Nearly every religious idea appears in a variety of forms, and . . . in the age to which the Enoch literature belongs there is movement everywhere."

Suppressing such a beloved book after it had circulated for five centuries and in many lands was more of a task than was anticipated by those who banned it—principally the Hilary who was Bishop of Poitiers from A.D. 353-367, the famous Augustine who was Bishop of Hippo from A.D. 395-430, and the great scholar Jerome, who left his home in Dalmatia (now Yugoslavia), went to Rome, and became papal secretary to Pope Damasus I, who commissioned him in A.D. 382 to make a new Latin translation of the Bible from the Old Latin, the Greek, and the Hebrew.

That Vulgate version, based on the long labors of Jerome, was finally completed in A.D. 405 and became the official Bible of Western Christendom for over a thousand years, and since Jerome had left The Book of Enoch out, it requires no expert sleuthing to deduce how the book got "lost"! But, in one corner of Christendom, over-looked by the censors, Enoch still lived on. We read the clue in chapter eight of "The Acts of the Apostles."

This book of Acts, by the way, which is really the second part of the Gospel of Luke, is now due for considerable reinterpretation in the light of the Essene Scrolls. The earliest Christian churches, especially those in Palestine, were in many respects more like branches of the Qumran Essenes than like the later Christian churches from the third and fourth centuries on. Scholars are now very busily but quietly at work on Acts. When they restore to the book certain omissions and delete a number of later theological insertions, the complexion of the document will be different. It is proof and a sample of the theological manipulations to which the book had been subjected that modern scholarship admits that the 37th verse of the 8th chapter is undoubtedly an insertion into the story of Philip and the Ethiopian eunuch of a baptismal formula first composed and used at least a century later.

When the eunuch wished to be baptized, Philip said, "If thou believest with all thine heart, thou mayest." And he answered and said, "I believe that Jesus Christ is the Son of God." So reads the 37th verse in the King James Version. But it is omitted in the Revised, American Standard Revised, and the new Revised Standard Version, because it is not in our four oldest Greek manuscripts, Codexes *Vaticanus* and *Sinaiticus* of the fourth century and Codexes *Alexandrinus* and *Ephraemi* of the fifth.

You do find the verse in the 1582 Rheims Version, the official Roman Catholic New Testament comparable with the King James Version used by the Protestants. But the latest Catholic New Testament, the 1941 Confraternity Revision of the Challoner-Rheims 1750 revision, puts the 37th verse in brackets, with the footnote, "Omitted in the best Greek and Vulgate MSS, and by other authorities."

We have taken this verse as a sample of "doctoring" of the Scriptures by the D.D. theologians, either by the insertion of words, phrases, and whole sentences, or by the elimination of others, in order to make the Bible prove the theological points they wished to make.

Now, the two-volume book, Luke-Acts, is the very core of the Christian Bible because it contains a key gospel and the earliest history of the infant Church, plus the Christian reinterpretation of the Jewish Old Testament, cleverly inserted in the form of several long sermons by Peter, Stephen, and Paul. In this important treatise many of these "doctored" passages have been recognized and admitted by modern scholars, who have restored the omissions and eliminated the interpolations, frankly noting them in most of the recent translations.

In confirmation of the elision of Enoch from the Christian Bible, there is one particularly interesting section in First Peter 3:18-20. In the King James Version it reads:

"For Christ also hath once suffered for sins, the just for the unjust, that he might bring us to God, being put to death in the flesh, but quickened by the Spirit: By which also he went and preached unto the spirits in prison; Which sometime were disobedient, when once the long suffering of God waited in the days of Noah, while the ark was a preparing, wherein few, that is, eight souls were saved by water."

This section has long puzzled Bible readers, and is not much clearer in the Revised Standard Version which has Christ "being put to death in the flesh but made alive in the spirit; in which he went and preached to the spirits in prison. . . ." The passage is simply saturated with theology in the process of formulation, as the rest of the chapter shows. Here, probably, is the origin of the creedal phrase, "He descended into hell," (the place in the recital of the creed where Queen Victoria is said to have crossed her fingers under her prayerbook), certainly a stumbling block for many Christians.

96

But Moffatt's translation of the 19th verse is: "It was in the Spirit that Enoch also went and preached to the imprisoned spirits. . . ." And Goodspeed has: "alive in the Spirit. In it Enoch went and preached even to those spirits who were in prison. . . ."

These three modern scholars were simply following the suggestion made by several Greek specialists—Bowyer, Spitta, Cramer, Rendel Harris, and M. R. James. Accordingly, it is obvious Enoch is the preacher meant and named in the original Greek; for in the Book of Enoch he preached to the disobedient spirits, and in chapters six to sixteen in that book the details are given about the "spirits" and why they were in prison "in the days of Noah." For these eleven chapters of Enoch explain and expand the first part of the sixth chapter of the Bible Book of Genesis in true Essenic fashion, like their Book of Jubilees (well named Little Genesis), and the recently diciphered roll from the first Qumran cave, erroneously named *The Apocalypse of Lamech*.

This motif of the "fallen angels," the "sons of God" who came down from heaven and mated with the fair "daughters of men" and were imprisoned for that sin, to hang in chains till Judgment Day (although the resulting children were said to be the "mighty men which were of old, men of renown" according to the King James Version), was a favorite legend among the Essenes, repeated and referred to many times in the Enochan literature and their other books, *Jubilees*, *The Testament of Reuben*, and *The Testament of Naphtali*.

The early Christians liked the story, too, and it is referred to several times in the New Testament, as we shall see later, and in the writings of the Church Fathers. It finally became the bone of contention between Tertullian and Augustine, for Tertullian maintained and supported his belief in the story by affirming the inspiration of the Book of Enoch, while Augustine denied the story. And since that denial was in the Bishop of Hippo's great book, *De Civitate Dei* ("The City of God"), it practically settled both the bad angels and Enoch for some time.

The dropping out of the name Enoch in First Peter 3:19 and the substitution of the pronoun "he," making Christ the one who "went and preached unto the spirits in prison," is accounted for by the scholars we mentioned (Harris, James *et al.*) as a scribal error known as "haplography," or writing only one of two identical groups of letters occurring near together. In the Greek MSS. ENOKAIENOK would mean "in which also Enoch . . ." But in the light of the systematic suppression of all evidence of the Essenic origin of Christianity, especially dropping any reference to the very significant name of Enoch, to blame its omission on a scribe seems too much like a politician attributing his unwise words to a reporter's or linotypist's error.

These "spirits in prison," the captive audience that theology took away from Enoch and gave to Jesus, were originally "sons of God" in the Hebrew of Genesis 6:2, but "angels of God" in the Alexandrine Greek Septuagint, and, variously, "the angels, the children of the heaven," or "the angels of God," or "the Grigori" (the Watchers) in the Essene books of *Jubilees, Enoch,* and the *Testaments of the Twelve Patriarchs.*

The Apostle Paul had his own opinion of these spirits in prison and knew, from his familiarity with the Books of Enoch that they were the "fallen angels" of Genesis 6:1-4, Isaiah 14:12 and 24:21-23, and particularly of First Enoch chapters 6 to 16, Second Enoch chapters 7 and 18, and Jubilees chapters 5 and 7. He was still suspicious of angels, principalities, powers, and all the ranks of intermediate beings. They might still hang around, waiting a chance to seduce the daughters of men, as in the passages mentioned.

Therefore, in his famous letter to the people in the church of Corinth giving advice in intimate matters, Paul says that any woman who has her head uncovered in church might as well have it shaven like a prostitute. All through the first part of that 11th chapter of First Corinthians he gives several rather vague and contradictory rationalizations as to why a woman should have her head covered in church while the men did not. Paul finally blurts out the real reason in verse 10: "Besides, for this cause ought a woman to have a veil upon her head, because of the angels." Women shouldn't tempt the angels by exposing their hair, which is their chief glory and attraction. As Paul reminded these same people in another letter: "Even Satan changes himself into an angel of light." (Second Corinthians 11:14).

The angelology of the Qumran Essenes as contained in their Dead Sea Scrolls throws a great light on Paul's beliefs and teachings, and Paul's rather superstitious fear of these suspicious celestial characters led him to advise all women to have a covering on their heads in church.

And women still do it, although few of them know why. I should know how deep-rooted is the superstition, for my innocent request in one pastorate during a large-hat-style period that the ladies remove their millinery (so that those behind them could see the charts I was using to illustrate a sermon) led the ladies to suggest firmly that the pastor would be removed before their hats were.

Besides the "descent into hell" phase in the Apostles' Creed and the "women-veiled-in-church" dictum of Paul, the Essenic story of the fallen angels who became "spirits in prison" was responsible, in its garbled version in First Peter 3:18-20, for still another doctrine that has caused much discussion among Christians and even today separates Protestants from Catholics.

For, later than Paul and Peter, the Church Fathers decided that some of these "imprisoned spirits" were

THE LOST YEARS OF JESUS REVEALED

ancient Jewish patriarchs who were kept in a "third place, or middle state of souls," and this passage in First Peter chapter 3, taken with its echo in the 6th verse of the next chapter, became the Biblical basis of the doctrine of purgatory, the alleged place or state wherein or whereby after death penitent souls are prepared for heaven by cleansing (purgation) of their sins through suffering and by the prayers of the living for the dead, also by the living giving alms and having masses said for the souls in puratory.

The Rheims (Catholic) New Testament has a footnote for I Peter 3:19 ("In which also coming he preached to those spirits that were in prison."): "See here a proof of a third place, or middle state of souls: for these spirits in prison, to whom Christ went to preach, after his death, were not in heaven; nor yet in the hell of the damned: because heaven is no prison; and Christ did not go to preach to the damned."

Father Ronald Knox's modern Catholic translation has a footnote here: "It is certain that this passage represents the holy patriarchs as living in a place of detention, neither heaven nor hell, till our Lord came. It is not clear why the Apostle concentrates his attention on the contemporaries of Noe (Noah)." Father Knox should have read I Enoch, chapters 12-16, or II Enoch, chapter 18.

Now, since The Book of Enoch was all too "informing" about the real origin of so many ideas, doctrines, and practices of the early Christian Church, and betrayed how the theologians had "interpreted," twisted, excised, interpolated, and even misquoted parts of the source documents, it is not difficult to understand why Enoch and all his tell-tale works, plus related apocalyptic and pseudepigraphic books similarly dangerous, simply must be excluded from the official canon.

But old Enoch is on his way back home now, after long exile, and should soon take his rightful place back in our Bible. For, if the Qumran community was the mother of Christianity, Enoch was the father.

11. The Story of the Ethiopian Eunuch

Enoch will return home. Like Ulysses, he has been a long time on his way back, and the saga of The Adventures and Return of Enoch is as romantic as that of the hero of The Odyssey. We can but summarize it here.

It really began with Philip the Deacon Evangelist and his encounter with the Ethiopian eunuch, a story on which much light is thrown by the Qumran cave discoveries. Indeed, this Bible incident alone, considered together with its implications, historical background, literary connections, and relation to the beginnings of the Christian Church, is likely to receive much attention in the near future, although it seems to have been overlooked so far by the Christian divines who assure us that the Scroll findings have not made one iota of difference to Christian theology!

The Bible story of Philip and the Ethiopian eunuch in The Acts of the Apostles 8:5-40 states that the eunuch was an important financial official of the court of the Queen of Ethiopia and was on his return trip after having worshiped at Jerusalem. When Philip, after a successful evangelizing and baptizing mission in Samaria, was directed by an angel to overtake the traveler, he found him reading a scroll of the Book of the Prophecies of Isaiah. The passage he was reading is quoted, the verses now numbered as 7 and 8 of the 53rd chapter, but it should be noted that they are given in the King James version of Acts exactly as they are worded in the

Septuagint Greek version of Isaiah. That fact is of considerable importance.

Philip explained the passage, one of the Suffering Servant sections of Second Isaiah, as referring to Jesus, and showed how Jesus fulfilled the other prophecies. As the chariot-riders came to a spring by the road, Philip baptized the eunuch at his request, "and when they were come up out of the water, the Spirit of the Lord caught away Philip, that the eunuch saw him no more: and he went on his way rejoicing." The miracle ending of the story is characteristic of nearly all narratives of the Apostolic period.

We have now reason to believe that the treasurer of the queen must have had Enoch as a very important passenger with him. For the treasurer had hardly made the long thousand-mile trip from Ethiopia merely to worship in the temple at Jerusalem. Whether he was a Jew in the service of the Queen of Ethiopia or a native Ethiopian who had become a Jewish proselyte, we are not told; perhaps he was neither. Nor are we sure he became a Christian, for if, with the best scholars, we leave out the Acts 8:37 verse about believing that "Jesus Christ is the Son of God," and note that nothing is said about his joining any church, he may have been, or may by the baptism have become, an Essene.

It was apparently true that the very early Christian movement, or pre-Christian group of Jesus-followers, was difficult to distinguish from a band of Essenes. For this baptism occurred before the conversion of Saul-Paul, and ten years before "the disciples were for the first time called Christians, in Antioch."

Reconstructing the probable course of events of the story of the Ethiopian eunuch, it may very likely have been that he came to the vicinity of Jerusalem for the purpose of visiting the Qumran community center and purchasing some of the scrolls that were being produced there, either as copies of old Hebrew scriptures or as new compositions, commentaries, anthologies, and translations. The wealthy and cultured Queen Candace may well have sent him on the long trip, amply supplied with gold for the purchases, to enrich her library and get information about the Essene center.

And if he was but one of a number of such purchasers coming from considerable distances to secure the valuable writings then being turned out in the very heyday of the Qumran publishers, the recently deciphered copper scroll of Cave 3, listing treasures of gold, silver and precious incense hidden by the prosperous Essene communitarians may not be merely telling tall tales, as is alleged by some of the always suspicious and incredulous scholars whom *Time* magazine calls "scroll snobs" (June 11, 1956 issue).

Corroborating the idea of the eunuch's probable connection with or at least interest in the Essenes of Qumran are several little items in the Bible account in the last part of chapter 8 of Luke's book, The Acts of the Apostles,—items now seen in the light of the cave discoveries to be of more importance than we had supposed.

Note, for one point, that it was Isaiah the eunuch was reading; in fact, Second Isaiah (the first 39 chapters are now called First Isaiah, and chapters 40-66, Second Isaiah), and still further, that it was the famous 53rd chapter which tells of "a man of sorrows, and acquainted with grief . . . despised and rejected of men . . . but he was wounded for our transgressions . . . by his knowledge shall my righteous servant justify many; for he shall bear their iniquities." This is part of the so-called "Suffering Servant" section, which has for centuries been believed by Christians to have been a direct prophecy, a prediction of the advent, suffering, and death of Jesus Christ, reverently called "The Man of Sorrows," from this very passage.

But the Qumran people apparently thought the 53rd

of Isaiah referred to their own beloved Teacher of Righteousness, especially the verse about "my righteous servant," which is even more applicable in the Revised Standard rendering, "by his knowledge shall the righteous one, my servant, make many to be accounted righteous; and he shall bear their iniquities."

At any rate, these Essenes certainly placed Isaiah very high in their canon. The first cave opened contained an almost complete copy and another fairly good one, and fragments of the book and of several different commentaries on it keep showing up as identifications continue. It will be remembered that it was from Isaiah, the 61st chapter, that Jesus read when he stood up in the synagogue, as told in Luke 4, where he said, "Today is this scripture fulfilled in your ears."

The fact that the eunuch raised the very point as to who this Man of Sorrow was ("of whom speaketh the prophet this?") might indicate that the identity of the Suffering Servant was already being debated, as to whether the prophecy referred to the Essene Teacher of Righteousness, or, as the new sect of Jesus-followers was now asserting, to their own Master.

And it was the eunuch who suggested the baptism ("See, here is water; what doth hinder me to be baptized?"), apparently out of a clear sky. Baptism was, at that time, even more featured among the Essenes than by the followers of Jesus, although he himself had been baptized by John the Baptist, who evidently made a specialty of it, as a symbol of repentance and preparation for the coming Kingdom of God. Just what was meant by Philip's baptism is hard to ascertain, for according to the first part of the same chapter it seems that Philip's baptizing methods were not satisfactory. His Samaritan converts "had only been baptized in the name of the Lord Jesus," and Peter and John had to come from Jerusalem and complete the process by the "laying on of hands" before the candidates "received the Holy Spirit."

It is very interesting to compare this idea in Acts 8 (that baptism is not complete without the receiving of the Holy Spirit) with the third column of the Rule of the Community or Manual of Discipline of the Qumran Essenes, where it is very distinctly stated that a man cannot be sanctified from sin by seas and rivers nor purified by any water for washing, but only "by the Holy Spirit of the Community, in His truth, shall he be cleansed of all his iniquities." (This is Dupont-Sommer's translation.)

One can hardly deny that Peter and John were following the Essene rule and adapting it to the emerging company of Jesus-followers, which was to become the Christian Church in due time.

When the Ethiopian eunuch rode off south on his way rejoicing, and whatever degree of validity and sanctity his impromptu immersion may have had, it is likely he learned from Philip on this trip, and probably from other Christian teachers later, enough about the new faith to give it a start in the court of Candace. Dr. Charles Foster Kent, in *The Work and Teachings of the Apostles*, page 63, states: "In a mind already prepared Philip sowed the seeds of the Gospel and thereby added to the rapidly growing ranks of the believers one whose influence may go far to explain why before the end of the first Christian century in distant Abyssinia there was a strong and flourishing Christian community."

Kent may be incorrect in identifying the Ethiopia of the time of Queen Candace with Abyssinia, but she may also have ruled the next section to the South (now the Sudan) and even part of what is now Abyssinia.

If a primitive type of Christianity did get as far as Abyssinia in the Apostolic Age, it may have dwindled, for the real evangelization of Abyssinia evidently took a fresh start early in the third century A.D. The Christian missionary Meropius of Tyre with two young men relatives started for the rather vague destination to the south then named "India," which even the Greeks located somewhere in Southern Egypt or Africa. On the western shore of the Red Sea their ship was wrecked, and Meropius was murdered by the Ethiopians, but the two boys, Aedesius and Frumentius, were taken to the palace of the king in Axum. They became popular and influential and the famous Christian bishop and theologian Athanasius of Alexandria consecrated Frumentius Bishop of Axum in A.D. 326. An Abyssinian type of Christianity, now known as Coptic, soon flourished.

The Roman Catholic church canonized the two young men, and still venerates Saint Frumentius and Saint Aedesius as the Apostles of Ethiopia.

Over fourteen centuries elapsed between the consecration of Frumentius and the momentous trip to Ethiopia of a canny Scot named James Bruce, who told the home folks that he was going to Ethiopia to try to discover the source of the Blue Nile, but he had a deeper motive. A Bible student, he had often wondered about the Book of Enoch, now so long lost. When he learned that the book had not been excluded from accepted Scripture until late in the fourth century A.D., and that Ethiopia had been evangelized early in that century, he wondered if perchance, due to the reverence of primitive peoples for the written word, there might not be still preserved in Abyssinia a copy of previous copies of Enoch translated long ago by St. Frumentius or other Christian missionaries into the Ethiopic language.

From 1768 to 1773 he traveled widely in Abyssinia and was so beloved by the people that he was made governor of one of the states. He found the source of the Blue Nile, followed it to its junction with the White Nile, and brought back with him accounts and a diary of his almost incredible adventures and three copies of the lost Book of Enoch in Geez, the ancient language of Ethiopia. But no one in England would believe his stories, and no one could then read Geez and translate Enoch into English!

Of the three manuscripts of Enoch, he gave one to the Royal Library of France, one to the Bodleian Library of Oxford, and the third was kept with his family records.

For nearly fifty years the important and precious manuscript lay neglected in Oxford, but in 1821 Dr. Richard Laurence, Professor of Hebrew there, published an English translation of the Bodleian manuscript, with the aid of a few collations from the "most magnificent quarto" manuscript in the Paris Library. The book was entitled *The Book of Enoch, an Apocryphal Production, Now First Translated from An Ethiopic Ms. in the Bodleian Library.* The title was enough to scare readers away. For all but a few scholars, the word "apocryphal" meant spurious, and who cared about Ethiopian manuscripts?

By 1853, when the great German scholar, Charles Friedrich August Dillmann, published his *Das Buch Henoch Ubersetzt und Erklart* (The Book of Enoch Translated and Explained), he had the benefit of five codices (manuscript volumes) of Enoch, and his book remained the standard work on the subject for forty years, although known only to German scholars and the few English ones who could or would read foreign theological books. By 1890, a scholar named Holtzmann had arrived at the conclusion that some sections of Enoch were of Essene origin.

In America, the only scholar who attempted to do a translation and commentary on Enoch was Professor G. H. Schodde of Capital University, Columbus, Ohio, but his book, published in 1882, was only a timid echo of Dillmann's and added nothing new.

Meanwhile in England, there was an atmosphere of worriment and concern about Enoch, for the more the book was studied, the more it became evident that there was an uncomfortably close connection between it and the New Testament. The Rev. William J. Deane, in his *Pseudepigrapha*, published in Edinburgh, 1891, wrote a long chapter on The Book of Enoch protesting that in a then-recent book, whose author and name he would not dignify by quoting (but evidently it was Renan) "we are asked to believe that our Lord and His apostles, consciously or unconsciously, introduced into their speech and writings ideas and expressions most decidedly derived from Enoch."

But Mr. Deane comforts his own readers by continuing: "Few unprejudiced persons will agree with the author of this opinion, whose aim seems to be to throw discredit upon the superhuman origin of Christianity and to trace it to merely human development. According to him, 'the work of the Semitic Milton was the inexhaustible source from which evangelists and apostles, or the men who wrote in their names, borrowed their conceptions of the resurrection, judgment, immortality, perdition, and of the universal reign of righteousness under the eternal dominion of the Son of Man.'"

But in two years there appeared the great work of Dr. R. H. Charles, *The Book of Enoch Translated from Dillmann's Ethiopic Text* (amended and revised in accordance with twenty more recently discovered and hitherto uncollated Ethiopic MSS., and with the Gizeh and other Greek and Latin Fragments), Oxford, 1893. And in this book Dr. Charles set forth in incontrovertible fashion the obvious influence, far-reaching and detailed, which Enoch had on New Testament doctrines and phraseology.

This was followed in 1913 by the huge two-volume set, edited by Dr. Charles, *Apocrypha and Pseudepigrapha of the Old Testament.* Twenty-seven of England's best scholars cooperated in the great project. The first volume dealt with the regular apocryphal books that once were printed between the Old and New Testaments in Protestant Bibles and that still are included in the Catholic Bibles (save First and Second Esdras and the Prayer of Manasses); and Dr. Charles also included Third Maccabees. All these books are presented in an English translation from the best critical texts of the original languages, with an explanatory introduction and a detailed commentary with critical and interpretative notes.

The second volume treats the pseudepigraphical books in the same fashion. The two volumes together comprise the first presentation in one work of a complete scholarly collection in English of the noncanonical Jewish literature from 200 B.C. to A.D. 100.

Just to glance through this second volume is something of a shock to a Christian unaware of this immense literature written just before and during the life of Jesus and his disciples, books which did not even get into the apocrypha, let alone the Old or New Testament, although many of the books were accepted as holy scripture by both Jew and Christian for centuries.

These are the books that built the frame of reference and furnished the thought-forms, idioms, vocabulary, doctrines, and ideas of Jesus and Paul and their contemporaries, much more than did the Old Testament books, with the possible exceptions of Isaiah, Deuteronomy, and the Psalms.

And these pseudepigrapha were among the books which were the Bible of the Essenes of Qumran! Moreover, of the Old Testament books, the Qumran community people preferred Isaiah, Deuteronomy, and the Psalms!

This is the important point about the "Dead Sea Scrolls," namely, that we have found the remains of the great library of the Essenes, and from its contents have discovered what some scholars have suspected: that the favorite books of Jesus and his disciples and early apostles were the very volumes that the Essenes loved best.

12. Squabble Over the Scrolls

It is not mere chance that the Scrolls that have best withstood the teeth of time and the raids of robbers are the apocalyptic Enochan group and similar pseudepigraphs and the books of Isaiah, Deuteronomy, and the Psalms.

These Scrolls survived because they were the best protected, not only by having been carefully packed, many of them, in sealed jars, but also because the most precious were hid in the smallest and least conspicuous caves. And Cave 4, where the greatest number were found and probably the ones they thought the most important, was cleverly chosen as the place where cave robbers would be least likely to search, the cave nearest the community center itself, with artfully concealed entrance.

The Seven Scrolls—the Manual of Discipline, the Habakkuk Commentary, the two Isaiah Scrolls, the Scroll of the Hymns, the Scroll of the Warfare of the Sons of Light and the Sons of Darkness, and the Midrash on Genesis 12-15, (wrongly called at first the Lamech Scroll) —are persistently called *The Dead Sea Scrolls*. There was some excuse for it at first, when these seven from the first cave were all that were then known and had, of course, received the enormous initial publicity; but it became inexcusable when a thorough examination of the first cave revealed fragments of many other ancient scriptures.

And especially now that many other scroll-bearing caves have been discovered, containing hundreds of manuscripts in various states of fracture (Cave 4 yielded literally tens of thousands of fragments), why confine the phrase *The Dead Sea Scrolls* to the seven first found by the Bedouins in Cave 1? The number of caves discovered near the Bahr Lut (Lot's Lake), as the Bedouins call the Great Salt Sea, is variously given as from 250 to 300, and the ones in which were found manuscripts and/or fragments thereof, as from a dozen to thirty, with a new one reported every few months.

Sections, at least, of all the books in the Protestant Old Testament have been found, with the possible exception of Esther.

What the general public apparently does not know, however, is that if you take all these "Biblical" book fragments and put them with the seven scrolls found in Cave 1 in 1945-47, you then have only a third of the "Dead Sea Scrolls" accounted for, since there is still left twice as much non-Biblical material. These books are not in our Bible now, but were, many of them, considered by the Essenes to be sacred scriptures, and were in the "Bible" of Jesus and Paul and Peter and John, and the early Church Fathers.

In this connection, a warning should be issued regarding the weasel word "original" which is so handy a semantic subterfuge. To many people, especially in America, the word "original" has come to have the derived, secondary, and additional meaning of "genuine," or even "the only genuine."

So, when any scholar or preacher or writer refers to the "original Dead Sea Scrolls," he may be referring simply to the first-found ones in Cave 1, but his audience or readers may take him to mean that those seven roll-books are the only really genuine Dead Sea Scrolls.

As a matter of fact, although those Isaiah scrolls found in Cave 1 are older by a thousand years than any manuscripts of Isaiah we had before, they are not "originals," but copies of a series of still older ones, written by more than one Isaiah, and edited into one book later, but before the time of the Essenes.

This matter of originality is confused in the public mind with both authenticity and authorization, and all three words are very loosely used. The King James or "Authorized" Bible of 1611 is by surprisingly many Christians still considered to be the "original" Bible, and all revisions thereof simply counterfeits forged by the "higher critics." Others, more educated but not well-informed, think the King James Bible is authentic and "authorized" in the sense of presenting the words of the authors of the books of the Bible, translated into English from the "original Greek."

The King James or "Authorized" Bible, however, was the third "authorized" and the seventh English Bible. It is true that the commission of scholars in six companies who sat down to revise the Bishops' Bible at the behest of King James in 1607 decided themselves to keep the readings of that Bible "as little altered as the truth of the original will permit." But the "original" texts they had to go by were very poor indeed. In the New Testament, for instance, they used the faulty Greek text of Etienne (1550 A.D.). The three best texts, all more than a thousand years older than Etienne's, were yet to be made accessible to Protestant Christians. The Greek or Eastern Church had Codex Alexandrinus and Codex Sinaiticus, and Rome's Vaticanus was not available outside the Roman Catholic faith until the nineteenth century. No wonder that the reconstructed Greek New Testament of 1881 (used by the English editors of the Revised New Testament) had almost 6,000 changes from the earlier alleged "original Greek," and one-fourth of these corrections change the sense of the passage.

Now this business of authorization, canonicity, authenticity, and originality of text has through the years become such a fetish that it has worked harm in two ways. First, it has become in the circles of the orthodox laity a great obstacle to the introduction of better readings in the new versions even when it is apparent that the proposed change makes the passage much more clear. In the second place, it has made the clergy and the Christian scholars and professors in theological seminaries reluctant to sponsor and champion changes in the text which they know very well are preferable to the old and accepted ones.

Already we see the same situation developing in regard to the Dead Sea Scrolls that we noted in the case of Mr. Deane, who protested sixty-five years ago, when the Book of Enoch was coming to public attention, that scholars were daring to suggest that "our Lord and His apostles" derived some of their ideas and expressions from Enoch! He said that they were evidently trying "to throw discredit upon the superhuman origin of Christianity, and to trace it to merely human development."

That is the point most frequently discussed today, when the issue is fairly faced and when the layman is permitted to ask questions. Was the origin of Christianity, or the advent of Jesus, a superhuman supernatural miraculous event, or was it a natural development in the evolution of human life and culture? Sometimes the question is condensed to "Was Jesus human or divine?" By which is meant, "Was he man or God?"

That is the real question, the crux of the whole dispute over the Dead Sea Scrolls. The laymen see the deity of Jesus Christ as the main issue, however much their spiritual leaders may or may not see it, or may avoid it or gloss it over. A thoughtful layman in a liberal church whose minister had preached on the Scrolls, reviewing Mr. Wilson's book, wrote me:

"When our minister spoke about the Dead Sea Scrolls, he said, among other things, that of course this book wasn't so important to the liberals as to others. By that

115

he meant that it wouldn't disturb their fundamental beliefs, *but* I reminded him of how important I thought it was because if it does remove from the general atmosphere some small part of the beliefs that a miracle happened in the Year One, that change in general belief *is* important to us as well as to anybody else." [Italics his.]

The so-called "War of the Scrolls" is not over: It has barely begun. For the lay public is still buying, reading, and discussing Edmund Wilson's popular little book, and people are not satisfied with the rather lame answers the theologians have given him. When the too-careful preachers get around to revealing to the public, in English, what has already been circulated in French au *mode savant* about the contents of the other caves, the second battle of "The War of the Scrolls" will begin to crackle in the columns of newspapers and magazines— and in Sunday School adult Bible classes!

For this whole dispute is the renewed rumbling of the ominous and insistent old question of the nature of Jesus, as to whether he was God or man, and the related question of the origin of the Christian Church. Was the phenomena a natural outgrowth of evolving ethical and spiritual Judaism, or a miraculous intervention in human history by God the Father sending His Son into the world "in the fulness of time" to redeem it and establish His Church, as Christianity has claimed for so many centuries?

Orthodox Christian leaders are obviously and understandably irritated, because they have considered the question of the deity of Jesus (and therefore the supernatural origin of Christianity) to have been settled long ago, after many decades of discussion in the great church councils. To any regular Protestant parson or Catholic priest this "squabble over the Scrolls" has seemed an unnecessary and objectionable rehashing of the old Arian-Athanasian controversy of the fourth century, which was decided at the Council of Nicaea in A.D. 325 and the Council of Constantinople in A.D. 381 in favor of the Athanasians who maintained firmly that Jesus was *homoousian* (of the same being or essence) as God, and against the Arians who believed he was *homoi-ousian* (of like being). Those councils were supposed to have settled the whole matter for all time.

This Arian early scientific interpretation of religion is not so remote from our subject of the Essenes and their religious literature as might be supposed. For Arianism can be traced from Arius the condemned heretic, banished to Gaul in A.D. 335, down to our day through such Arian missionaries as Ulfilas whose teachings converted the Goths and Teutons (and eventually the Anglo-Saxon English). And that idea of a more naturalistic religion can also be traced back in history from Arius straight to Jesus and the Essenes.

Arius was born in A.D. 256. He received his education in that Antioch in Syria where the disciples of Jesus were first called Christians, probably because of their Essenic emphasis on the Messianic-Christian doctrine of the Coming Kingdom of God and the Son of Man.

Antioch was important in Arius's education, for there he sat under the teaching of the great Presbyter Lucian, a very learned man and noted scholar who revised the Greek Septuagint Old Testament by comparison with the Hebrew text. And Lucian was, in turn, a follower of Paul of Samosata, the famous "heretical" Patriarch and Bishop of Antioch, excommunicated by seventy bishops, priests, and deacons for teaching that Jesus was a man who became God, rather than a God who became man.

Now, this doctrine of Patriarch Paul's affirmed that what Mary gave birth to was not the Logos (the Word), but a man; not the Creative Wisdom of God which became the Second Person of the Trinity, but Jesus, who

117

was good, yet a mere man like other men until he received the Holy Spirit at John's baptism, whereupon he reached such a degree of holiness that God adopted him as His Son. Naturally, this doctrine was soon named Adoptianism, although sometimes referred to later as Humanitarianism.

Tracing this Adoptianism of Arius, Lucian, and Paul of Samosata further back, we find Theodotus of Byzantium and his follower Artemon teaching Adoptianism in Rome about A.D. 185. Before that, it flourished among the Ebionites, a rural Jewish sect of the first and second centuries A.D., who seem to have included survivors of both Essenes and Palestine Christians, after the fall of Qumran and Jerusalem in A.D. 70 had disrupted both religious groups.

So a form of Adoptianism, or belief that Jesus was only human until he was adopted by God the Father at his baptism (some said his resurrection), was apparently the current belief in Palestine in the first century A.D. and well into the second, among certain Christians, especially around Antioch.

13. Origin of the Doctrine of the Holy Spirit

The finding of the Dead Sea Scrolls has also brought into the spotlight the most complicated, least understood, and most vulnerable doctrine of the Christian Church, the Holy Spirit, the Third Person of the Holy Trinity. For it now begins to look as if the study of the Essene idea of the relation of baptism to the coming of the Holy Spirit of Truth may supply the clue to the origin of the Christian doctrine and perhaps lead to its simplification, or even its eventual elimination.

For the Adoptianist theory that Jesus became the Son of God through the visitation by the Holy Spirit, not at his conception or birth by Mary, but when that Spirit descended on him at baptism "like a dove," has textual as well as traditional authority back of it.

In the passages in the Christian Gospels (Matthew 3:16-17; Mark 1:10-11; Luke 3:22) which tell of the descent of the Holy Spirit and the coming of a voice from heaven saying, "Thou art my beloved Son (or my Son, the Beloved); in thee I am well pleased," several ancient manuscripts as well as quotations in the Church Fathers (Justin, Clement, Origen, Augustine) support the reading in the "Gospel of the Ebionites" in Luke 3:22, which runs: "Thou art my Son; today I have begotten thee."

That reading has finally made its way into the margin of Luke 3:22 in the Revised Standard Version. Some day, when Christian scholars are more courageous, it may get back into the regular text, where it probably was originally, as a direct quotation from Psalm 2:7, a favorite verse in New Testament times, quoted verbatim in Acts 13:33 and Hebrews 1:5 and 5:5. Albert Huck's scholarly "Synopsis" restores the Adoptianist reading to the text of Luke 3:22.

This Adoptianist (and Essenic) ending of the heavenly proclamation was evidently changed from "today I have begotten thee" to the trite and harmless "in thee I am well pleased" when the early Christian theologians were removing traces of Essenism and abandoning the doctrine of Adoptianism under the influence of the trend toward the dogma of the Virgin Birth, a more acceptable theory among the Gentiles, who were familiar with it in other religions as one of the common popular proofs of deity.

When the Qumran manuscripts are properly recognized and evaluated in relation to the books in our very much edited and expurgated New Testament, the doctrine of the Holy Spirit will have to go, and will take with it the doctrine of the Trinity, which never was in the New Testament anyway. The only proof text stating this peculiar belief in the union of three in one, called "the ineffable mystery of three persons in one God—Father, Son, and Holy Ghost," was First John 5:7, "For there are three that bear record in heaven, the Father, the Word, and the Holy Ghost: and these three are one."

But that verse was a forgery, a deliberate interpolation, said by some to have crept in from a marginal note, and has been so recognized, for it was eliminated by the English revisers in 1881, by Moffatt, Goodspeed, and the editors of the recent Revised Standard Version. The King James and Rheims (Catholic) versions retain it. But the Confraternity (Episcopal-Catholic) version, while retaining it in the text, has an eloquent footnote, admitting that "According to the evidence of many manuscripts, and the majority of commentators," the verse should not be included, but "The Holy See reserves to itself the right to pass finally on the origin of the present reading."

In the Qumran community, according to the Manual of Discipline, when a man entered he was baptized, but it was not the water that cleansed him from sin. The water baptism was not of any avail unless the candidate had also the Spirit of Light and Truth in his soul. His "iniquities will be atoned" when he "looks upon the Light of Life" and he will be cleansed from his sins "through the Holy Spirit of Truth" which "will direct his steps so as to walk perfectly in all God's ways."

Jesus was apparently echoing and clarifying this Essene teaching at the time he told his disciples they would receive the Holy Spirit, and promised "when he, the Spirit of Truth, is come, he will guide you into all the truth."

The Essene baptism did not count unless the prospective member truly meant and had a feeling consciousness of the significance of the rite—that is, unless he was really honest and truthful about it. And Jesus probably expected no more than that of his own disciples.

But by the time the early Jerusalem church got well started, the "Holy Spirit" was looked upon as a real ghost or spirit, supernatural and magically powerful, which took possession of a person at baptism. Soon it was taught that the Holy Spirit had come down from heaven and entered Jesus at his baptism in the form of a dove.

The descent of the Holy Spirit upon Jesus at his baptism, which the Adoptianists, at least, believed to have been the time God "begot" Jesus (rather than at the Virgin Birth or Virgin Conception), led to the expectation that anyone joining the group of Jesus-followers by "following the Lord Jesus in baptism" would immediately show in some way that the Holy Spirit had entered into and "possessed" him.

That evidence must appear, else its absence was interpreted as proof that the baptism had not been a valid one, and some important apostle, say Peter or John (Acts 8:14-17), would have to lay hands on the candidate and thus magically transfer some of the apostolic mana or power of the Holy Spirit into him.

The evidence of the presence of or "possession" by the Holy Spirit was some "spiritual gift," not at first in the sense in which we understand the phrase today, but miraculous and supernatural abilities and talents such as "speaking with tongues," the sort of ecstatic unintelligible utterances which psychologists today call "glossolalia."

Other miraculous *charismata*, or charisms, as these miraculous gifts or talents are called by theologians, were instantaneous cures and healings, exorcism or the casting out of demons, prophecy in the sense of prediction or precognition, the ability to receive visions and revelations when "in the spirit," and the valuable "gift" known as the "discerning of spirits." This talent was supposed to enable the *hermeneut*, or interpreter, to discern whether the voices speaking through the person in trance or babbling in unknown tongues were the voices of demons (evil spirits) or of angels (messengers of God, like the Holy Spirit).

Paul is the great New Testament authority on all these miraculous charismata. He devotes three chapters (12-14) in First Corinthians to an elaborate explanation of these "spiritual" phenomena, besides rather veiled references in his letters to the Romans (chapter 12) and the Ephesians (chapter 4).

Anyone familiar with the various phenomena of spiritualism and the modern psychological explanations of ecstasy, possession, compulsions, transference, projection, and other evidence of the activity of the unconscious, will recognize the symptoms Paul describes.

This idea that it had to be an apostle who laid his hands on a convert at baptism, if it was a true baptism of the spirit as well as a water baptism, played a very important role in the evolution of Christian doctrine as it emerged from its Essene background. In Samaria Philip had "preached the gospel news about the kingdom of God and the name of Jesus Christ," and the Samaritans, both men and women, had believed and were baptized. (Acts 8:12.) But when Peter and John went on a sort of follow-up mission to Samaria, sent by the leaders of the Jerusalem group, they prayed for the new Samaritan converts and "laid their hands on them and they received the Holy Spirit." (Acts 8:17.)

In this incident we note how three later Christian doctrines got their start, the doctrines of the Holy Spirit, the Trinity, and Apostolic Succession.

The Holy Spirit, or Holy Ghost, evidently grew out of the early church's gradual build-up into a vague personal metaphysical spirit, nebulous but powerful, from Jesus' frequent references (according to the Fourth Gospel) to the Spirit of Truth which would guide his disciples into all the truth.

Jesus' "Spirit of Truth" phrase and idea most probably reflects the Essene "Holy Spirit of Truth" referred to in their Manual of Discipline as previously noted by us, which was certainly very different from the later Christian Holy Spirit, the third Person of the Trinity. Just what Jesus and the Essenes meant by the Holy Spirit of Truth we may know better when more scroll fragments are translated. In the 9th column of the Manual of Discipline a passage referring to the "Institution founded by the Holy Spirit for Eternal Truth" seems to mean the whole Qumran Community itself. At times, when reading the Manual carefully, one gets the impression that the Holy Spirit is synonymous with Truth, or Righteousness, or Justice, and that the Essenes were struggling hard to express and emphasize the importance of this abstract idea without personifying it enough to make it a rival of God.

Perhaps what they were trying to say would be put this

way today: Being baptized by water into the Community of the New Covenant is not enough. That doesn't wash away your sins. You must really mean it in your heart. In the Spirit of Truth is the only way to enter this Fellowship of Truth and Justice.

Whether Jesus meant any more than that when he spoke of the Spirit of Truth that would guide his disciples into all the truth, we do not know. According to the Fourth Gospel, he referred repeatedly (John 16:13-15) to this Spirit of Truth as "he," which is certainly personification and to a greater degree than in the Essene Manual.

For in the Manual, a long section (column 3, verse 13 to 4:26) is inserted, rather out of context, describing the Two Spirits in Man—the Spirit of Truth and the Spirit of Perversion. And while these spirits are referred to as the Angel of Darkness and the Prince of Lights or the Angel of Truth, nevertheless they are neither of them called "he." The neuter pronoun is used. "The one of them God has always loved, forever delighting in all its deeds. The other He was always loathed, forever hating all its ways."

So it may be that Jesus went a little farther toward personifying the Spirit of Truth than his Essene teachers had, as he apparently had no compunction about changing what he got from any source, whether from the Teacher of Righteousness or Moses. "Ye have heard that it was said to them of old time . . . but I say unto you. . . ." Or, on the other hand, it may have been the writer of the Fourth Gospel who did the changing, while Jesus meant by the Spirit of Truth just what the Essenes did.

There is, however, in this semipersonified Holy Spirit of Truth, or Justice, or Righteousness, and particularly in the Essene Spirits of Truth and Perversion, the Angels of Light and Darkness, a singular similarity to the gods or high angels of the Persian Zoroastrian pantheon. The seven archangels whom Zarathustra (Zoroaster) saw on his visit to heaven were all personified virtues.

To Zoroaster, Light and Truth were practically identical

and were personified in Ahura Mazda; while Darkness and Untruth were one in the person of Angra Mainyu, also called "The Prince of Lies," "The Lie Demon," and "The Lord of Evil and Darkness."

If any serious student of pre-Christian Jewish literature has hitherto doubted the Essenic origin of Enoch and the other pseudepigraphic writings that so frequently illustrate the eternal ethical conflict by the symbol of light versus darkness, thus faithfully reflecting Persian Zoroastrian influence, he must surely now admit that the Qumran cave Essene scroll well-named The War of the Sons of Light and the Sons of Darkness, as well as the long section of "The Manual of Discipline" describing The Two Spirits in Man (the spirits of light and darkness), prove the point beyond the flicker of a doubt.

Like a Zoroastrian priest intoning a verse from the sacred *gathas* (hymns) of the *Avesta* (scriptures), the Qumran Teacher of Righteousness might have been heard at sunrise chanting:

"In the wellspring of light is the birthplace of truth; But from the womb of darkness come the children of error."
(The Manual of Discipline, column 3, verse 19)

In another Essene book, The Testaments of the Twelve Patriarchs, (Judah, chapter 20:1) the same idea appears: "Know therefore, my children, that Two Spirits wait upon man—the Spirit of Truth and the Spirit of Deceit . . ." and Dupont-Sommer remarks that this is the first appearance in Jewish literature of the theme of the Two Spirits, and bears "the definite mark of the Jewish Sect of the Covenant." (*The Jewish Sect of Qumran and the Essenes*, p. 130.)

But another and perhaps earlier Essene book (First Enoch) speaks several times of the spirits of light, and in one passage comes even closer to the central thought of the passage just quoted from the Manual. First Enoch 108:11-12 reads: "And now I will call forth the spirits of the good who belong to the generation of light, and I will transform those who were born in darkness . . . and I will bring forth clad in shining light those who have loved My holy name. . . ." This Enochan passage is in a final chapter that has been considered by some to be an appendix to the book and of different authorship, but it is distinctly Enochan in tone and language. Similar verses mentioning "every spirit of light" and "the light of the Lord of Spirits" are found in First Enoch 61:12 and 38:4. And Second Enoch 30:15 has God saying of Adam: "And I gave him his free will, and I showed him the two roads, the Road of Light and the Road of Darkness, and I said to him: 'This one is good and that one is evil . . .'"

So Zoroaster's dualism of Light versus Darkness, as a sort of visible symbol or dramatization of the conflict between Good and Evil, was seized upon by the Essenes, especially by the Teacher of Righteousness, as an excellent metaphor, and the coming great and presumably final struggle between the forces of righteousness and the forces of unrighteousness became The War of the Sons of Light with the Sons of Darkness.

14. Prophecies of "The Last Days"

No one can read that War Scroll from the Dead Sea caves without recognizing that it is the forerunner, the prototype, and in its vivid imagery the partial source at least of the final book of the Christian Bible, the Apocalypse, or Book of Revelation.

In the War Scroll, as in the Christian Apocalypse, we are in the Land of Imagination, beholding a vision of bloody conflict which is at times a nightmare, an orgy of hatred and anger and smiting and vengeance. In both these books of cosmic crisis, we constantly hear clamor, shouting voices, and trumpet sounds. In both, the magic number seven is featured again and again. The Book of Revelation has fifty-eight "sevens" in it—seven churches, seven angels, seven seals, seven stars, seven candlesticks, seven trumpets, and so on. The Warfare Scroll tells of seven lines of horsemen, seven hundred on each side, of seven lances, of seven Levites holding seven rams' horns.

"The seven angels which had the seven trumpets" in the Book of Revelation, chapter 8, verse 6, are definitely pre-figured in the 7th column of the War Scroll where seven priests clad in white linen sound their trumpets.

On these trumpets, according to column 3 of the War Scroll, are to be written many different inscriptions, evidently considered the messages which the horns were to blast forth to the enemy, challenges such as "The Hand of God Powerful to Smite Down the Faithless," and "The Powers of God for Routing the Enemies of Righteousness."

127

By the time the Christian Apocalypse was written, this quaintly poetic idea of the trumpet itself proclaiming a message of its own had been carried further toward personification. Instead of merely bearing an inscription, the trumpet had miraculously acquired a voice. In the first chapter, beginning at verse 10, the author of the Book of Revelation states:

"I was in the Spirit on the Lord's Day, and heard behind me a great voice, as of a trumpet, saying, 'I am Alpha and Omega, the first and the last': and 'What thou seest, write in a book. . . .' " And that this word "trumpet" is no mere figure of speech, but is meant to suggest something more, is shown by the first verse of the fourth chapter, where the author says:

"After this I looked, and, behold, a door was opened in heaven: and the first voice which I heard was as it were of a trumpet talking with me; which said, 'Come up hither, and I will show thee things which must be hereafter.' "

Now, when John heard a "voice" that sounded as if a trumpet were talking to him, a Bible student would be immediately reminded of the story in the nineteenth and twentieth chapters of Exodus, the account of the "voice of the trumpet exceeding loud" coming from the thick cloud on Mount Sinai, which "waxed louder and louder," shaking the whole mountain, until "Moses spake, and God answered him by a voice," and then dictated to Moses the Ten Words, called the Ten Commandments.

The people were so frightened by the trumpet voice that they begged Moses not to let God do it again. But the idea gradually grew among them that God would speak with that terrible trumpet voice once again, shaking not only the mountain, but the whole earth, and that would be the end of the world and Judgment Day. We find references to this idea in the prophets Joel and Haggai, but it developed very rapidly in the time between Malachi and Matthew. The Essene books are full of the teaching of the coming end of the age and the advent of the Messiah, the coming of the Son of Man on the clouds of heaven. The sure sign of the arrival of the Messiah would be the trumpet voice from heaven. The Last Trump should announce the New Covenant just as the First Trump at Sinai had proclaimed the Old Covenant. The Essenes were expecting that day to come very soon, and so were the early Christians, even before they were named Christians or Messianists.

In a very real sense, since the word Christian means Messianist (the Greek word Christos being the exact equivalent of the Hebrew word Messiah, meaning the anointed one), and since the Essenes were very much concerned with the coming of Judgment Day and the Messiah, they were Messianists; and, to use the Greek form of the word, they were Christians before Jesus Christ was born. The fact that later generations of the followers of Jesus filled the words "Christ" and "Christian" and "Christianity" with complicated theological meanings, adding more and more doctrines for several centuries, until being a "Christian" meant believing a complex system of dogmas that the Jewish Jesus never heard of, does not alter the fact that when his disciples were first called Christians at Antioch in Syria, they were Christians much like the Essenes were, or any pious Jew who was waiting in earnest expectation of the Messiah.

After Jesus had died and his followers became more and more sure that he was indeed the real Messiah, the Christ of God, they began thinking about the prophecies of Judgment Day, and the New Covenant, and that trumpet voice. The twelfth chapter of the Epistle to the Hebrews is an attempt, and a very good one, to reconcile the known facts with the prophecies. In it the author decides that Haggai's prophecy of the great second shaking at the sound of the trumpet voice has been fulfilled (evidently by the earthquake in Jerusalem when Jesus was crucified, Mount Zion thus succeeding Mount Sinai) and that Jesus is thereby the mediator of the New Covenant.

The Epistle to the Hebrews, long attributed to St. Paul, has by many been assigned to Apollos, and by others to some unknown woman. Lately, however, according to the London Unitarian *Inquirer*, there has been quite a stir raised in England by some who have maintained that the "Hebrews" to whom the letter was written, were the Jewish Essenes of Qumran! That would be rather difficult to prove, but there are several arguments in favor of the supposition, such as the emphasis on the priesthood of Melchizedek, King of Salem, priest of the Most High God, "King of Righteousness, and after that also King of Salem, which is, King of Peace." (Hebrews 7:1-2.)

This Melchizedek, mentioned in the fourteenth chapter of Genesis, and in the 110th Psalm, is said in Hebrews 7:3 to have been "Without father, without mother, without descent, having neither beginning of days, nor end of life; but made like unto the Son of God; abideth a priest continually."

Since the author of the Letter to the Hebrews identifies Jesus with this Melchizedek ("We have such an high priest, who is set on the right hand of the throne of the Majesty in the heavens"; Hebrews 8:1), calling Jesus also "holy, harmless, undefiled, separate from sinners," it is not difficult to guess where the doctrine of the Virgin Birth may have received its initial impulse.

The entire epistle is full of phrases and ideas that we are constantly meeting in the Essene literature; and since it is written in the best literary style and most nearly correct Greek of the entire New Testament, it may well have been written not *to* the Qumran Essenes necessarily but very possibly *by* one who had been trained among them by their great scholars and rhetoricians.

15. The Kingdom of Heaven and the Empty Tomb

The theory that the Qumranians were vegetarians, so hipped on the idea of strict dietary purity that they abstained from the Temple sacrifices lest they be suspected of countenancing the eating of flesh, has received quite a jolt with the discovery of a great heap of animal bones in the monastery backyard. They raised sheep and cattle for food, as we've mentioned before. So, those who have been saying that Jesus could not have been a Essene because he was not an abstemious monk shut up in a monastery away from the world, but so mixed in with men of all sorts that he was accused of consorting with publicans, sinners, and even harlots, are likely to play that note more pianissimo as growing evidences of the actual world-awareness of the powerful sect of the Essenes gradually become known. The notion that the Essenes lived in poverty and deprivation is on the way out, as excavations, identifications, deciphering, and translating proceed to reveal, for instance, the treasure recorded on the copper scroll.

Individually, it is true, the Essenes of the Salt Sea Shore owned nothing; but the community itself, by the time of Jesus, was very wealthy. When one joined it, he did give all his worldly goods to the "poor," as Jesus advised the rich young ruler to do, who "turned away sorrowful for he had great possessions." But, at Qumran, as at Jerusalem in the days of Ananias and his wife Sapphira, the "poor" meant the members of the New Covenant community.

131

There are three different Greek words in the Bible which are translated "poor" and eleven Hebrew words so rendered in the King James Version, ranging in actual meaning all the way from lean, weak, needy, and impoverished to humble, hungry, and oppressed. And there are several other words meaning poverty, which was apparently something else.

In the four gospels—Matthew, Mark, Luke, and John—especially in the Beatitudes (which, as we shall soon show, are typically Essenic in origin and content), and in the Psalms of David, as well as in the apparently Essenic Psalms of Solomon and the Gospel Beatitudes the word "poor" frequently has a religious meaning or connotation, more than an economic one. Sometimes it seems that "poor" means "good" and "rich" means "wicked."

This Essenic background explains the Lukan version of the Beatitudes spoken by Jesus, where he says, rather cryptically, "Blessed, ye poor: for yours is the Kingdom of God," (Luke 6:20), and (verse 24) "Woe unto you that are rich, for you already have what gives you consolation."

Matthew modifies the saying, either to soften it or interpret it, rendering the saying: "Blessed the poor in spirit: for theirs is the kingdom of heaven." Matthew, always a cannier public relations man, is careful to omit the Lukan woes.

Note particularly that both Matthew and Luke state that Jesus said that the "poor" already *have* the Kingdom of God, or Heaven. That idea is an apocalyptic concept, an Essenic emphasis.

What Jesus was saying was simply that the members of the Essenic messianic communities of the New Covenant were *already* living in the blessedness of God's Kingdom of Brotherly Love. In his emphasis on the present tense ("theirs *is* the kingdom of heaven") he could not have been talking to "Christians" as we think of them today, but rather of the "Messianists" of Qumran and similar folk who were following him as he taught certain truths which were partly Essenic in origin but were slowly changing in pattern.

Jesus' own teaching, his doctrine, his personal belief, as far as we can discover it by disentangling it from the words which gospel writers and later theology-minded editors so obviously put in his mouth, never did become the dogmatic trinitarian neo-Gnostic system which Paul and his successors constructed out of what the twelve apostles and other disciples remembered Jesus to have said and done. Paul, in fact, never limited himself even to such sources, knowing them to be enthusiastic rather than responsible reporters, and often contradictory; but supplemented these oral traditions by drawing on his various psychic "visions" and "voices," as Mohammed later did, and also by using helpful ideas from the other faiths, cults, and "mysteries" of the time, as was the cheerful custom then (and still is) among canny and uninhibited religion-makers.

Remember that Paul, in shaping up his Christology (his theory of the relation of Jesus to God and man and history), was not handicapped by having to make it conform to the King James version of the Gospels of Matthew, Mark, Luke, and John, or the Acts of the Apostles. All his "epistles" were written before the earliest manuscripts of the Gospels and Acts appeared. It is doubtful also if he ever saw the pre-gospel collections of the teachings, parables, and healing miracles of Jesus—documents supposed to have been the sources, in part at least, of the four canonical Gospels.

Modern scholars specializing in the field of New Testament origins have named these the "Q," "M," and "L" documents, and the "Urmarcus," along with the "Logia" (sayings) which have been more or less recognized for some decades. These so-called "higher critics" have laboriously and cleverly reconstructed these alleged "sources" of the four canonical Gospels from the quotations, peculiar verb-forms, case endings, vocabulary, ideas, doctrines, historical background, and frames of reference still distinguishable, so they claim, in the Greek and Latin manuscripts of the Gospels, although those books are supposed to have been written originally in Aramaic!

It should be remarked that there is as yet no general agreement among the scholars themselves as to the extent and content of these conjectural pre-Gospel sources, and many of the long dissertations in journals, quarterlies, and books are more ingenious than convincing.

The fact that Paul probably never saw either the Gospels or their literary sources, if any, since all his epistles were written earlier, leaves us to infer that he was dependent on oral tradition, the word-of-mouth accounts of those who had known Jesus; so his brief summing up (in First Corinthians 15) of the death, burial, resurrection, and post-resurrection appearances of Jesus includes no details. Indeed, he throws considerable doubt on the actual physical manifestation of Jesus to the disciples when he classifies those post-resurrection appearances with his own experience on the road to Damascus, which included psychic voices and a "heavenly vision."

Scholars have for some years been making an important point of Paul's making no mention of the empty tomb which all the gospel writers feature as proof of the resurrection of Jesus. These modern scholars have implied that since Paul wrote earlier than the four evangelists, the empty tomb story was invented and/or developed by them to corroborate the other stories of his rising from the dead.

But since Paul tells the whole story of the death, burial, resurrection, and appearances in six short verses, his silence concerning the empty tomb is a weak argument; nor does it at all prove that the vacant sepulchre tale is fictional. As Professor J. Spencer Kennard Jr. of Benedict College says: "When stripped of supernaturalism the empty tomb may point rather to a removal of the body from the place where the women had seen it laid and its burial elsewhere." (*Journal of Biblical Literature*, vol. 74, 1955, p. 227.)

As all of us know, Matthew 28:11-15 states that the Jews said that Jesus' disciples came by night and stole him away, and that "this saying is commonly reported among the Jews until this day." Justin Martyr, somewhat later, states that the Jews sent emissaries "throughout all the world" to teach that the disciples "stole him by night from the tomb where he was laid when unfastened from the cross." The Catholic scholar Loisy thought that the body was cast into the "Field of Blood," and others assume that Joseph left it in the tomb during the Sabbath and then took it elsewhere.

Professor Kennard has worked for twenty years on the problem of "The Burial of Jesus" and has had the help of several eminent scholars in weighing and evaluating the contradictory and confused Gospel and Pauline stories. His considered opinion after this careful and exhaustive research and study is that "in the light of these facts and probabilities," liberal scholars have been too hasty in rejecting the empty tomb stories, and even though those stories did get assimilated to the resurrection visions, we do not have to think the empty tomb was an inference from the visions. So he concludes his long study with the statement: "Thus when Jews spread abroad the story that the disciples of Jesus had 'stolen' the body, they spoke the truth."

16. The Question of the Ages

Was Jesus God, or man, or perhaps both?

For almost twenty centuries nations and races east and west, kings and emperors, priests and bishops, preachers and people have bitterly argued and fought over this tremendous question, often to the loss of life and fortune, and in ways not always sacred or honorable.

Now suddenly, in our day, the dramatic discovery of the long-hidden Dead Sea Scrolls in the Qumran caves has raised the ghost of that same old never-quite-solved problem, and in a most unexpected and very challenging form.

The Christian Church, of course, had long since settled the question to its own official satisfaction. It has proclaimed for centuries that this Jesus was God's own and only begotten Son, sent from heaven to Palestine by His Father to be born miraculously of a Jewish virgin, to grow up and reveal by word and deed God's plan of salvation by suffering and dying on the cross to atone for the sins of the world, and then to rise from the dead and, after showing Himself alive for forty days, to ascend back to heaven to sit in glory at God's right hand, whence He will eventually come again at the Last Judgment to judge, reward, or punish all people then alive and all who have previously died.

Those who believe this (and several other related teachings, for additions are occasionally being made, even in the twentieth century) and join the church by baptism and profession of faith will be saved, and go to heaven; but those who persistently refuse will be *ipso facto* (by their very refusal) self-condemned to hell.

The best-known short statement of this basic church teaching is found in the Gospel of John (3:16) "For God so loved the world that he gave up his only son, so that anyone who believes in him may not perish, but have everlasting life."

Jesus is said to have carried out his Father's plan of salvation completely; and today devout pilgrims are shown the Bethlehem Grotto of the Nativity, the cave-stable where he is said to have been born of the Virgin Mary nearly twenty centuries ago. Then, not far away, just outside Jerusalem, they are shown Joseph of Arimathea's cave-tomb where Jesus was temporarily buried after his crucifixion on Golgatha.

The event of Jesus' birth is considered to have been so momentous, and such a decisive break into history, miraculously ushering in a new age or period of time, the Christian Era, that we now reckon our years from that date, so that A.D. (anno Domini) 1962 means "In the 1962nd Year of Our Lord."

But however epochally important Jesus' earthly advent may have been or may have been considered later (and it would be difficult to think of any event more noteworthy historically whether one deems him God or man), it is certainly unfortunate that no one seems to have made an accurate record of it. The Gospel accounts are sadly confused.

When the B.C.-A.D. device was first used in A.D. 533 to designate the advent of Jesus and the Christian Era, the sixth-century monk Dionysius Exiguus did the best he could, but we know now that he made an error of several years.

In the nineteenth century, when it became evident and was finally admitted that Herod died in the year 4 B.C., and it was recalled that, according to the story in Matthew's Gospel (2:16), King Herod, in order to eliminate

137

little Jesus as a possible "King of the Jews," had ordered all infants of two years old and under to be killed, the birth-date of Jesus obviously had to be moved back to 4 B.C. at latest. Today, scholars prefer 5 to 6 B.C. as the date best accommodating the inconsistent and even contradictory traditions, legends, and gospels, although some historians push the date back to 8 and 10 B.C.

The problem of the correct dating of Jesus' birth, life, and death has now been raised again (due to several statements in these Essene Scrolls) along with the related question of his deity. Some people are wondering if perhaps he even lived a century earlier than we have thought.

Strangely, but quite appropriately, it is the discovery, thirteen years ago, close by the birth-cave and the burial-cave, of a third cave, the contents of which have lately focused critical attention upon this beloved "Son of God." A third cave, yes, and then hundreds of caves, some with thousands of manuscripts and fragments, which suddenly demand the reappraisal, revision, and even correction of much we have taken for granted about the Bible and Christianity, and probably about Jesus himself.

For, as we have seen, from these caves of Qumran have come manuscripts referring to a great spiritual leader, a Master of Justice or Teacher of Righteousness, a commanding figure whose description makes any Bible student think at once of Daniel's night vision of "one like the Son of Man." A coming Messiah is also often mentioned in the Scrolls: some scholars identify two different messiahs. But the Teacher of Righteousness seems not to have been officially recognized as a messiah, although that point is not very clear.

But, Messiah or not, if the Teacher of Righteousness was killed by his enemies, possibly crucified, about the year 688 U.C. (*Urbs Condita*, Latin for the founding of the city of Rome, believed to have been 753 B.C.), that would figure out as 65 B.C. for the death of the great Qumran teacher.

Hence, knowing that the date of the birth of Jesus has been necessarily pushed backward in time recently, as we have learned more about his contemporaries and his times through research and excavations, some historians have been considering the possibility of there having been a confusion between the two men in the minds of their followers, with a blending of traditions. The nearer together in time they lived, the more the likelihood of that. And we do know that they lived in the same country and that their homes were within a few miles of each other. Indeed, the opinion that Jesus either lived for several years in the Qumran community which produced the Scrolls or at least visited it often is gaining ground among unprejudiced students.

And as scroll after scroll is unrolled and bushels of priceless fragments are sorted and deciphered, it is seen more and more clearly how much this strange unnamed Man of Destiny, the Teacher of Righteousness, resembled in many ways the man Jesus, while at the same time he differed so much from the Christ-God of the later theologians and the churches that the religious (and historical) importance of the Qumran findings can hardly be overemphasized.

For, in the light of these Scrolls, their contents and particularly their pre-Christian origin, there must take place a radical and thorough review, restudy, and revaluation of extremely important matters such as the education, beliefs, parentage, deity, and even the existence of the unusual person named Jesus, called Christ, together with the related problems of the origin, founders, liturgy, doctrines, and early literature of the Christian Church. And especially those scriptural books rejected when the "canon" of Old and New Testament books was gradually and finally established.

The radical reconsideration of all these important ideas and doctrines in the light of the Scrolls is our duty in spite of the opposition of vested theological interests and institutions, whose representatives apparently are already trying desperately to conceal or at least minimize the importance of the manuscripts.

The ardent defenders of the faith once delivered to the saints (defenders whose loyalty we can appreciate even while we question their judgment and methods) are apt to concentrate their fire on the Teacher of Righteousness, perhaps because they see that this anonymous figure has caught the admiring attention of the general public.

It may be that this Qumran leader's brief biography, with additional items we have not yet discovered, became the literary foundation of Christianity. That seems improbable, but the possibility must be carefully explored. It is more likely that Jesus, who was evidently very familiar with the books of the Qumran library, patterned his own career and teachings in part after this great religious leader, teacher, and martyr. Certainly Jesus' teaching, especially the Sermon on the Mount, and the writings of his followers which together make up The New Testament resemble closely in both vocabulary and ideas the contents of many of the Qumran cave manuscripts.

Now, if Jesus followed in the main the customs and teachings of this community, still flourishing in his day as it had for at least a century before, it is apparent that the later Christian theology which made him the Son of God, miraculously sent down from heaven, was simply the product of the exaggerated enthusiasm of his followers. It was worshipful enthusiasm over the very fine character and personal magnetism of a noble man who took the best teachings of the men of old and of his own time and blended them with some of his original splendid inspirations into a message of love and peace and hope for mankind.

His own people, the Jews, said and still say that Jesus was a man, a teacher, a prophet, a healer of the sick. They say he was a good man, but if he or his followers thought he was God, or the Son of God, he and they were terribly mistaken; for it is not only an error, but blasphemy, according to the strictly monotheistic (One-God) Jewish religion, to say that a man can be God, or that God could have a son!

But Jesus' early followers, including at first some Jews, gradually came to believe that he was the Christ, the expected Messiah who should save the Jews from their enemies and restore the kingdom of David. Jesus, however, had interpreted that Messiahship quite differently. Not as a warrior king like David had he come, but as a Christ of Love and Prince of Peace.

After his death, his followers insisted that he was even more than that. They said he had risen from the dead after his crucifixion, had been seen by many during forty days, and then had ascended to heaven in a cloud to be with his Father.

Before long they were saying that Jesus had been with God before the foundation of the world, but that God had loved the sinful old world so much that He had sent His only son down to save it, to suffer and die on the cross as a sacrifice atoning for the sins of the world, and rise on the third day in victory over death itself!

And the Christian theologians said that whosoever believed this, and testified to his belief by being baptized into the Christian fellowship, would have his sins forgiven and would not perish but have everlasting life like his Saviour Jesus Christ, whom he would join in the heavens where Jesus had gone to prepare mansions for all good Christians. Whosoever did not believe this would go to hell, the bishops said.

But there were always those, even among the Christians, who questioned parts of this scheme of salvation and damnation, especially the transformation of the gentle Jesus, the Man of Galilee, into a God who would send any human being to hell forever.

Then for centuries, Christians debated how and to what degree Jesus partook of the nature of God, and how

much of him, if any, was man. They not only debated—
they even killed one another over this question of
whether the Prince of Peace was God or man! Finally,
the creed-makers decided that Jesus was both God
and man.

Even today, in spite of all we have learned during the
centuries between in comparative religion and anthropol-
ogy, about virgin births and men-gods in earlier "heathen"
religions, that old official decision still holds. The National
Council of the Churches of Christ in the United States
of America refuses to admit into its membership churches
of the Unitarian and Universalist denominations because
their members do not believe in the godhood of Jesus.
The National Council does not consider that one who
follows Jesus and tries to live up to his teachings is a real
Christian unless he also believes that Jesus was God. Since
Unitarians, like the Jews, reject the doctrine of the deity
of Jesus, they have often been called "Jewnitarians."

It must not be overlooked that the great majority of
the people on the earth, despite nineteen centuries of
Christian missionary activity, do not believe Jesus was
God. People of other ethnic faiths, such as Confucianists
and Buddhists, consider him to have been a great teacher
and prophet, but a man, not a god. And the reason why
Moslems resent being called Mohammedans is that, as
they carefully point out, "We of Islam are monotheists,
people of One God, like the Jews. We honor Moses and
Jesus as prophets. And we honor our Mohammed as the
greatest prophet, but we do not worship him; we worship
only one God, Allah."

There are, too, many millions of perfectly respectable
persons, including scientists, philosophers, physicians, edu-
cators, and other professional people, living in Christian
countries, who do not believe that Jesus was God simply
because they doubt the existence of any gods, devils,
angels, or other supernatural beings.

Nevertheless, there are, according to their own statistics, three-fourths of a billion baptized Christians of various kinds on this planet, one whole third of the inhabitants thereof; and at least ninety-nine-and-nine-tenths per cent of them profess to believe that Jesus was God incarnate.

Down underneath the professed belief, however, there have been doubts among many thoughtful Christians, some of whom have given token or surface allegiance to the church for the sake of family, business, or "respectability." And now those latent smoldering doubts have apparently been fanned into flame by the epochal finds in the caves of Qumran.

Some of the clergy and certain orthodox "scholars" have accordingly rushed to steady the "Ark" by making public statements, soothing and reassuring in phrase and intent but of very questionable accuracy, statements they will regret when they have "bothered" to read carefully even the few of these amazing documents already available. These "defenders of the faith" (some very obviously without examining the evidence), have been too quick to presume that nothing could possibly have been unearthed that would upset in the slightest any Christian doctrine, or change the Bible.

Apropos of this we recall that just one of the newly discovered manuscripts was responsible for fifteen changes in the text of the book of Isaiah, quietly inserted at the last minute in the new Revised Standard version.

The widely heralded and acclaimed "return" of religion and the churches has probably been due not so much to the attractions of theology, which interests lay people very little even when they understand it, but more likely to the new and growing fascination of the study of the psychology of personality, hence the quickened interest in the greatest personality of all time. Whether we approve of the trend or not, we are blind and deaf if we do not recognize that psychology is rapidly gaining on theology, if not superseding it, as the attraction, explanation, and dominating factor in modern religion.

And the reason why people the world over are so very much interested in the Qumran manuscripts, so dramatically brought to light, and why they will be for a long time asking keen questions about the finds, is the hope that somewhere in them there may be found or implied the secrets of personality development, perhaps learned by Jesus in these hidden and so-called apocryphal books and imparted by him to his disciples who so often "understood not the things which he spake unto them."

Those disciples and the theology-obsessed Church Fathers who followed them were so anxious to deify Jesus and build up a system of philosophical theology that would send their enemies and doctrinal opponents to hell, and would assure themselves front seats in heaven, that they tragically overlooked his real significance. They did admit that "he knew what was in man," and that he lamented their childish infatuation with miracles and the supernatural ("Except ye see miracles and wonders ye will not believe"), but they missed his big message—*that they could do the same things he did!* They missed, too, the psychosomatic character of his healings. Rather than think deeply and observe carefully what actually did take place, they preferred the easy explanation of the mentally lazy, and used the fuzzy blanket-word "god" to cover their ignorance.

The first-century followers of Jesus and the theologians and their successors can be excused to some extent for failing to perceive that he was no god come down from heaven, but rather a very great human being, ahead of his time in his intuitive understanding of his fellows and in his apparently instinctive knowledge of the technique of what we now call psychotherapy. They can be forgiven, for they had not studied psychology, as had the early followers of Gautama the Buddha, who preached salvation by the psychological suppression of vain desires. And it

144

should be noted that the early disciples of the Buddha did not deify him, although he lived and died five centuries before Jesus.

But the present-day followers of Jesus, and modern Christian theologians, living in a day when the knowledge of the principles of psychology is available to almost anyone who cares to learn them, have no excuse for using the very limited and inadequate thought-forms of the Palestine people of two thousand years ago to explain the personality and character of this splendid leader and teacher of men, who was perceptive, keenly intelligent, sympathetic, comprehending all the vices, virtues, and motives of humans, a man who took the best he had read and thought, and interpreted it to humanity by embodying it in his own life.

He demonstrated truth, he incarnated righteousness; but that did not prove he was a supernatural being. It is Jesus the Man who understood men, whom men want to know and have always wanted to know. And the Scrolls from the Salty Sea fascinate us because they may throw some light on what he studied and thought and what his radiant personality really was before the theologians made a god out of him.

To anyone who keeps abreast of discoveries of bits of parchment and papyrus which are, or claim to be connected with the beginnings of Christianity, the 1945 Chenoboskion finds, especially the one called "The Gospel of Thomas," are exceedingly interesting. For, between 1897 and 1903, there had been found in Egypt three fragments, known as the three papyri of Oxyrhynchus, numbered 1, 654, and 655, and known popularly as the Oxyrhynchus Sayings of Jesus. The largest (number 654) of these three fragments had long ago been torn through the middle, and the "cross-word puzzle" for many theologians in the six decades since has been to try and complete the half-lines of the document. Surprisingly, they seemed to have done so.

But the exhuming and translating of "The Gospel of Thomas" from the Chenoboskion-Nag Hammadi funeral urn proved that "gospel" to be no gospel at all, but a collection of over a hundred of the Sayings of Jesus, and the Oxyrhynchus #654 page once contained in Greek the beginning of the collection of Sayings, of which the newly-found "Gospel of Thomas" is a Coptic translation. Furthermore, the theologians' clever restorations were far from correct.

There have been (up to 1962) three English translations of the "Sayings" miscalled "The Gospel of Thomas," and they vary greatly. Jean Doresse in "The Secret Books of the Egyptian Gnostics" counts the Sayings as 118. The Grant-Freedman-Schoedel "The Secret Sayings of Jesus" reckons them as 112. The Guillaumont, Puech, Quispel, Till, and 'Abd Al Masih book, "The Gospel According to Thomas," gives the number as 114. The variance is due to differing decisions as to where to split up the meandering sentences.

Many of the sayings are obviously the same as some of Jesus' words in the canonical gospels, with slight variations. Others vary greatly, but are recognizable. Still others start out having a faint resemblance, but switch off to a Gnostic slant or interpretation. About half seem to be pure Gnosticism, but may have been based on words of Jesus of which the orthodox gospel writers knew or said nothing. The most that Christian scholars have yet admitted is that the author, or editor, or collator of the Thomasian sayings may have had access, among other sources, to the same collections of the *logia* (sayings) and/or *agrapha* (unwritten sayings in oral tradition) of Jesus as did the authors of the Bible gospels. But, of course, the defenders of orthodox Christianity will always maintain that the Gnostic writers of the vast known-of (but mostly destroyed) Gnostic literature changed, perverted and misused the original words of Jesus. Probably they did. But that the Christian "fathers" also did so is increasingly apparent to careful students as more information becomes available. What Jesus actually did say and do is still to be determined with exactness, but already it is becoming apparent that he was far more eclectic and selective than either the orthodox or the liberal scholars supposed.

Jesus' sayings, aphorisms, proverbs, and beatitudes (now called "macarisms" by modern scholars), whether found in the collection known as "The Sermon on the Mount" or elsewhere in canonical scriptures or in non-canonical writings, number at least two hundred, and who is yet wise enough to say which ones are genuine? And he seems to show in them his careful selection from Judaistic, Essene, Persian, Alexandrian Greek, Gnostic, Syrian, and even Pythagorean sources. Then he rearranged, restated, and transmuted them through his own original personality and experience until those who heard him and followed him, even afar off, caught enough of his radiant religion to pay him the highest tribute their limited vocabulary knew. They deified him, in spite of his protest "Why call ye me good? There is none good but one, that is, God."

17. Essenism and Christian Gnosticism

There is somethig unusual and coincidental, almost what once was called "providential," in the fact that the "Dead Sea Scrolls" or, better, the Qumran Essene manuscripts, and the Gnostic codices found near the ancient town of Chenoboskion, once a monastic center and famous for its cemeteries and crocodiles, were both discovered in the same year, 1945. The modern town of Nag-Hammadi is near the site, and "Library of Nag-Hammadi" was the name first given to the Gnostic volumes but Dr. Kendrick Grobel's suggestion (page 8 in his 1960 book, *The Gospel of Truth*,) that the codices, 49 Gnostic books bound in thirteen volumes, be called "Library of Chenoboskion," seems more appropriate.

First reports had the story that, like the Bedouins of the Dead Sea area, the natives discovered the books while hunting through caves for valuable guano deposits, accumulated from birds and bats through the centuries. In an almost inaccessible cave halfway down a vertical cliff, reached by letting a man down by a rope from the top of the precipice, they found a large jar, in which, almost perfectly preserved, were a baker's dozen of leather-bound volumes, some hand-tooled, with envelope-like flaps and thongs to tie the books safely. It was said that the unlettered fellahin used two of the volumes as fuel for making tea, and sold the rest for the (to them) incredibly high price of three Egyptian pounds, about $8.50. Only one of the volumes has as yet left Egypt, and that clandestinely. It was smuggled to Belgium, taken to the

United States, and almost sold here. Then it went back to Belgium and disappeared. In 1952, a Belgian resident of Zurich named Page found and bought it, allegedly for $5,000, and presented it to the Jung Institute of Zurich, where it now abides as the papyrus Codex Jung.

The Jung Codex contains five books: namely, an apocryphal Letter of James, a Letter of Rheginos on the Resurrection, a Treatise on the Three Natures, a fragment of a prayer supposedly by an apostle, and "The Gospel of Truth." The last named has already been translated from the Coptic and published with notes and introduction by Dr. Kendrick Grobel, professor of New Testament at Vanderbilt Divinity School and translator of the two-volume *Theology of the New Testament* written by the great German theologian, Dr. Rudolph Bultmann, Dr. Grobel's father-in-law.

Dr. Grobel subtitles his book "A Valentinian Meditation on the Gospel," that is, on the Christian Gospel, the "Good News" of salvation, brought by the Master Teacher, Jesus. The Christian Gnostic Valentinus who wrote "The Gospel of Truth" was born about A.C. 100, and is not to be confused with the famous St. Valentine who was martyred in Rome about A.D. 270, allegedly on February 14th. In the much later centuries St. Valentine's Day was appropriated by lovers for the exchange of tokens of affection, since it was supposed to be the day when birds mated.

But our earlier Valentinus was a very brilliant Christian scholar, educated at Alexandria. He and Basilides (who flourished in Alexandria from A.D. 125 140 and wrote poems and the Exegitica, 24 books of Gnostic commentary on the Bible) were probably the best-known and most influential teachers of Gnosticism in the second century.

All the 44 Gnostic books, after the five in the Jung Codex were sold, were seized in 1952 by the Coptic Museum in Cairo, and of this great Library of Chenoboskion, only one volume of 158 photographic plates had been published in 1960. A further parallel between the Qumran Caves find and the Gnostic discovery is the delay in making the manuscripts available to scholars and translations thereof to the Christian clergy and laymen. And confused reports, contradictory of previous announcements, come from both sources. The Chenoboskion story now current states that the large pottery jar of books was found by laborers making an excavation who accidentally dug into a fourth-century Christian tomb. But soon Chenoboskion must match Qumran by bringing a goat into the legend. Eventually Dr. Bultmann will be hired by the scholars in both places to demythologize the discovery narratives.

A Dutch scholar, W. C. van Unnik has just published, translated from the Dutch, a paperback called *Newly Discovered Gnostic Writings*, wherein he gives a list of the 44 books in Cairo, as revealed by Dr. Peuch in the *Encyclopédie Francaise*, and by Jean Doresse in his book *Les livres secrets des Gnostiques d'Egypte*. The latter has been translated into English by Philip Mairet and published by Viking Press.

From the titles alone of these books one can judge what a potpourri of ideas, doctrines, and superstitions are here assembled, and even infer the nature and character of the literary contents. Van Unnik well names it "a motley array of bizarre titles" and remarks several peculiarities, such as "the absence of any books of a historical character," and, more unusual in a collection of Christian religious books, "the absence of any manuscripts of biblical books!" Yet, the titles claim the documents have "connections with apostles" and "include revelations of the Lord Jesus." These are all apocryphal but do not correspond to any of the many titles in Montague James' *Apocryphal New Testament*. And in this Christian collection there are several treatises of the non-Christian

Hermes Trismegistus school of alchemy, astrology, and the generally occult.

Dr. van Unnik warns us not to be deceived into thinking that books with the same title are necessarily the same. Doublets are not always duplicates. He says that "not everything that appears to be the same is so in fact: the title, Revelation of James, occurs three times, but these three writings have nothing to do with one another." Some of the thirteen codices contain six or seven books: others only two or three. They are given by Dr. van Unnik as arranged and numbered by Puech, but with Doresse's numbering in brackets. But I have condensed and abbreviated wherever possible, and have arranged the codices according to the number of titles, putting the more inclusive ones first. Whatever order they may have been in when packed in the large jar, (really a fire-proof urn), that order was surely lost when the fellahin laborers first wrenched it open and—to their great disappointment, for they had hoped for gold or jewels—"out tumbled a number of manuscripts." And there must have been further disarrangement by the time, ten years later, that the Coptic Museum finally established legal possession of all the codices, which had arrived in three separate lots. History was repeating itself. Whereas the Qumran treasures were unearthed in the midst of political conflict between Jordan and Israel, the Gnostic Codices turned up in Egypt against the equally stormy background of King Farouk's deposition by Naguib's revolutionaries, and Nasser's subsequent take-over. Strange that the two greatest discoveries of literary treasures known to Bible archaeology should have been complicated and even imperiled by religious quarrels! In Palestine, the real squabble was (and is) between Jews and the Moslem Arabs; and in Egypt the rising nationalism of that Moslem country was suspicious of interference by "Westerners," meaning particularly French Catholic Christians.

Speaking of the disarrangement of the codices, there

turned up at Cairo eventually the "lost" section of the Jung Codex, much to the relief of the Zurich Jung Institute, whose benefactor, Mr. Page, it is now stated, paid, not five, but ten thousand dollars for a supposedly complete codex, of which a large part proved to be missing. We hope this will not prove to be a *casus belli* between Switzerland and Egypt! We are glad to report, however, that through Dutch influence the Egyptians were persuaded to make the Chenoboskion codices accessible to scholars as quickly as possible, this apparently in return for an agreement whereby the Jung Codex will eventually be returned to Egypt to make complete the whole collection in the Cairo Coptic Museum.

Eminent Egyptian, European, American and English scholars, specialists in the many Coptic dialects and authorities on Gnosticism, are already at work editing and translating the prized manuscripts. Eventually, photographic reproductions of these books will be available to the scholars of the world. Here is the list:

(1) Apocryphon of John, Gospel of Thomas, Gospel of Philip, The Hypostasis of the Archons, The Exegesis Concerning the Soul, The Book of Thomas (Secret Words Spoken by the Saviour to Judas Thomas and Sealed by Matthias), and An Anonymous Revelation, dedicated to Pistis-Sophia.

(2) Acts of Peter, Authentic Address of Hermes to Tat, The Thoughts of the Great Power (Simon Magus?), three Hermetic Treatises, (all without title, and all different), and a Sethian Revelation (without title).

(3) Apocryphon of John, The Sacred Book of the Great Invisible Spirit (or The Gospel of the Egyptians), Epistle of the Blessed Eugnostus, The Wisdom of Jesus, The Dialogue of the Saviour.

(4) Epistle of the Blessed Eugnostus, Revelation of

Paul, Revelation of James, Another Revelation of James, Revelation of Adam to his son Seth.

(5) (THE JUNG CODEX) Revelation (Apocryphon) of James, The Gospel of Truth, Epistle to Rheginus concerning the Resurrection, Treatise upon the Three Natures.

(6) Paraphrase of Shem (Second Treatise of the Great Seth), Revelation of Peter, Teachings of Silvanus, Revelation of Dositheus, or The Three Pillars of Seth.

(7) Revelation, attributed to the Great Seth, Epistle concerning the Father of the Universe and Adam the First Man, Treatise in epistolary form, Treatise (without title) against the Scribes and Pharisees concerning the Baptism of John.

(8) The Threefold Discourse of the Threefold Protennoia, Sacred Book written by the Father, Revelation in the form of an epistle.

(9) The Exposition of Gnosis, The Most High Allogenes (Stranger), Revelation of Messos.

(10) Revelation (without title), Discourse on the truth of Zoroaster (?), Epistle of Peter to Philip.

(11) Apocryphon of John, The Sacred Book of the Great Invisible Spirit.

(12) Fragments of a treatise on the cosmos.

(13) A compilation discussing various moral questions and the Influence of Daemons on the Soul.

Lest we should undervaluate Gnosticism because its terms, symbols, and vocabulary differ so from ours, it should be stated that Gnosticism was Egyptian Christianity for the two hundred years that the leaders of the new faith were working out its theology. It was gradually pushed out by orthodox Catholic Christianity and its books were burned. Similarly, Essenism was the early form of Palestinian Christianity and its Enochan apocalyptic literature was ultimately destroyed. But, at Qumran and at Chenoboskion, hidden for centuries, were the great libraries of these early forms of Christianity, which now so suddenly and dramatically have been restored to us. And Essenism and Gnosticism were much alike: if you doubt it, read the canonical Gospel of John, especially the first chapter, where you will find both Essenism and Gnosticism, blended with and sublimated into the Christianity more familiar to us.

And both have survived apart from orthodox Christianity until today, in the religious movements known as Rosicrucianism, Anthroposophy, and Theosophy, and, less obviously, in Christian Science, Religious Science, and New Thought.

Epilogue

The discoveries are continuing on the shores of the Salty Sea, and will for some time as the Bedouins bring in their fragments of precious manuscripts, bits of leather now become trade currency.

But we already have enough data to show that the Scrolls are really "God's Gift to the Humanists," for every unrolling reveals further indications that Jesus was, as he said, "The Son of Man," rather than the deity "Son of God" his followers later claimed.

What the laymen suspect regarding the cave finds is true. The dogmas and doctrines, the theological twists and turns, the tampering with texts to corroborate newly invented creedal statements, all these additions of later centuries to the simple ethical humanitarian faith of Jesus the Teacher of Righteousness are revealed by these older Scroll manuscripts to have been like the tawdry tinsel and bright-colored finery with which ignorant peasants adorn the statues of their gods.

For Jesus the Galilean, baptized by John Baptist into the great fellowship of the pacifistic, socialistic, cooperative Essenes of the New Covenant, later evidently carried out in its principles into the wide world, improving those principles in some respects, but preaching them best by living up to them to the limit, even to death on the Roman cross.

One leading Christian theologian, having discovered my knowledge of the contents of the Scrolls and their eventual and inevitable effect on the history of Christian origins and church doctrine, said to me rather wistfully the other day:

"Well, Doctor, I see you *know*." Then he added, slowly "I don't know what we're going to tell our dear people!"

"You'd better tell them pretty soon," I ventured, "for some of them are beginning to suspect. And what will you tell them when you do?"

"Personally," he said, "I've decided to break it gently by saying that the Scrolls reveal that there were three or four Essene sects in Palestine in Jesus' day, of which all died out but one, which is now popularly known as Christianity."

Index